Black Bears

A Natural History

Dave Taylor

Fitzhenry & Whiteside

Black Bears: A Natural History
Copyright © 2006 Dave Taylor

Fitzhenry and Whiteside Limited
195 Allstate Parkway
Markham, Ontario L3R 4T8

In the United States:
311 Washington Street,
Brighton, Massachusetts 02135

www.fitzhenry.ca godwit@fitzhenry.ca

Fitzhenry & Whiteside acknowledges with thanks the Canada Council for the Arts, and the Ontario Arts Council for their support of our publishing program. We acknowledge the financial support of the Government of Canada through the Book Publishing Industry Development Program (BPIDP) for our publishing activities.

 Canada Council   Conseil des Arts
for the Arts   du Canada

Library and Archives Canada Cataloguing in Publication
Taylor, Dave, 1948-
Black bears : a natural history / Dave Taylor.
Includes bibliographical references and index.
ISBN 1-55041-849-1
1. Black bear. 2. Bears. I. Title.
QL737.C27T394 2006   599.78'5   C2006-901888-X

United States Cataloguing-in-Publication Data

Taylor, Dave, 1948-
Black bears : a natural history / Dave Taylor.
[192] p. : col. photos. ; cm.
Includes bibliographical references and index.
Summary: A complete examination of the North American Black Bear.
ISBN 1-55041-849-1 (pbk.)
1. Black bear – North America. 2. Bears. – North America. I. Title.
599.78/5   dc22   QL737.C27L39 2006

Book design by Fortunato Design Inc., Toronto

Printed and bound in Hong Kong

1 3 5 7 9 10 8 6 4 2

Contents

Acknowledgements

First, I'd like to thank all the various biologists and researchers across the continent who so willingly shared their research with me, either through correspondence or their websites. Virtually every state and province supplied me with their bears' current status, including Iowa whose letter simply stated, "No bears here." These scientists are too numerous to mention by name but I greatly appreciate their time and effort. The bibliography at the back of the book acknowledges the work of many of them.

I am especially grateful for the help and guidance of Dr. Martyn Obbard, an Ontario predator biologist, who welcomed me several times to participate in his field research.

I would also like to thank Bill and Klari Lea. Their remarkable bear-viewing spot is worth a book all of its own. I'm certain one day they will get around to writing one.

My thanks go as well to those who accompanied me on my bear trips: Don McClement, who spent a few hours with me at a dump near Algonquin Park and joined me on my first trips to view bear research first hand; Jim Markou, who travelled to Katmai, Denali, Yellowstone, and Waterton Lakes to seek out the bears; Gary Hall, who photographed his first black bears with me; Dean Wyatt, who hosted my daughter and me at Knight Inlet Lodge; Arthur Dejong, who shared his vision of peaceful coexistence with bears in Whistler; and Ken Kingdon and Pat Russo who taught me about Manitoba's bears.

My wife, Anne, does not much like bears. We had one knock over our tent once in Jasper, and she saw me chased into a car on more than one occasion in Yellowstone in the early 1970s. She was terrified as we watched a big black bear eat our pork and beans while on our travels along the Alaska Highway. For all that, she has accompanied me into bear country more than anyone else. She has seen almost as many bears as I have and, in her own way, has come to enjoy the animals too.

My daughters, Liza and Ashley, have seen only a few bears, but they're hooked too. It is always a delight to share wildlife with your kids, and I look forward to more of this in the years to come.

Some researchers need special mention. George Kolenosky is known worldwide for his work on Ontario's bears. Randy Sequin, a bear biologist for the Saskatchewan Wildlife Department, freely shared information, as did Tom Edwards, District Wildlife Biologist for Kentucky. Thank you all.

Other professional photographers have crossed my path from time to time. Some took the trouble to advise me, though I doubt they remember me, but I remember them and appreciate their help. Thanks to John Morrow, Bill McRae, Tom Teitz, Jim Fowler, John Mitchell, Andy Russell, and the late Tommy Thompson. I try to do the same for those budding naturalists and photographers that I meet along the way.

I would be remiss in not expressing my appreciation to Canon Canada for supplying all cameras (film and digital) and lenses. Most of this book was photographed using Kodachrome, and I am grateful for Kodak Canada's support. However, I have, like many others, gone to digital.

I would also like to express my sincere thanks to my editor, Anita Levin, and to Richard Dionne and Amy Hingston at Fitzhenry & Whiteside for all their support.

I have tried to portray the world of the black bear honestly and accurately. I hope this book captures some of the wonder and awe I felt in the presence of these animals and the people who work with them.

Introduction

In 1990 I embarked on a quest to photograph and research the bears of North America. It has taken me from the Canadian tundra to the swamps of Florida and from the east coast of the continent to the west. The more I travelled, the more I realized there is no end to what I could see and learn. The photographs and information in this book cannot begin to portray all there is know, but it is time to share my experiences.

North America is home to three species of bears: the grizzly or brown bear, the polar bear, and the black bear. Black bears are by far the most numerous of the three species, and they live closest to people. If you are to encounter a bear, it will most likely be a black bear.

Because I live in Ontario, where the population of black bears is large, I have observed many and found them to be fascinating crea-

tures. They are misunderstood animals, though. The sight of a black bear in the neighborhood usually arouses serious safety concerns, if not downright terror, among local residents. But there really is very little to worry about. Black bears are by nature shy, reclusive animals that normally avoid people. On the other hand, they are big, naturally well-armed animals, and fairly intelligent. This combination can lead to dangerous encounters and, very rarely, deadly ones.

The black bear is a complex animal. My goal in writing this book is to provide the reader with a greater understanding of the bear and its habitat so that curiosity and respect takes the place of fear. I was not an idle witness but became actively involved with my subjects. I hope this book encourages others to safely bear witness too.

PART I: The Evolution of the Black Bear

The black bear (*Ursus americanus*), also known as "the American bear," is the only bear species found exclusively in North America and the only one to evolve here. The common ancestor of all bears is first found in the fossil record over 30 million years ago, and all living bears, except the spectacled bear and the giant panda, share a common ancestor that was established 5 million years ago. Ancestral bears that eventually evolved into the modern black bear had crossed the Bering Land Bridge from Asia over 3 million years ago, and by 500,000 years ago the modern form of the black bear was in existence. The other two species found in North America, the polar bear and the grizzly (brown) bear, are recent immigrants—they crossed over from Asia only about 100,000 year ago.

Brown (Grizzly) bear

Sloth bear

Malaysian Sun bear

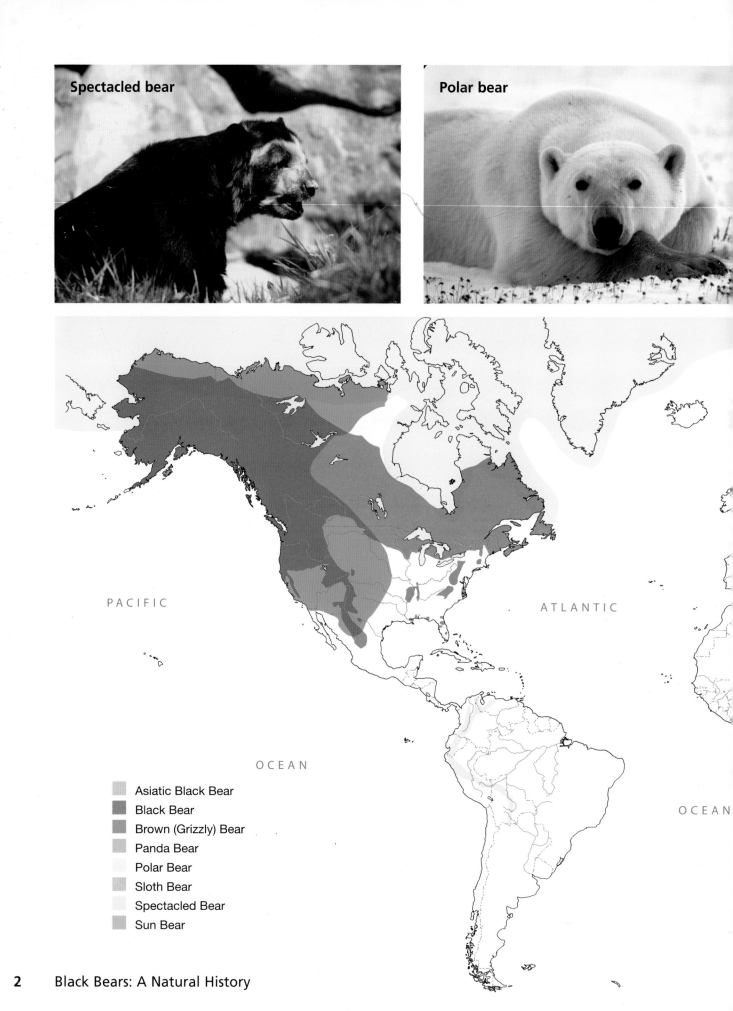

Spectacled bear

Polar bear

PACIFIC

ATLANTIC

OCEAN

OCEAN

Asiatic Black Bear
Black Bear
Brown (Grizzly) Bear
Panda Bear
Polar Bear
Sloth Bear
Spectacled Bear
Sun Bear

Panda bear

Asiatic black bear

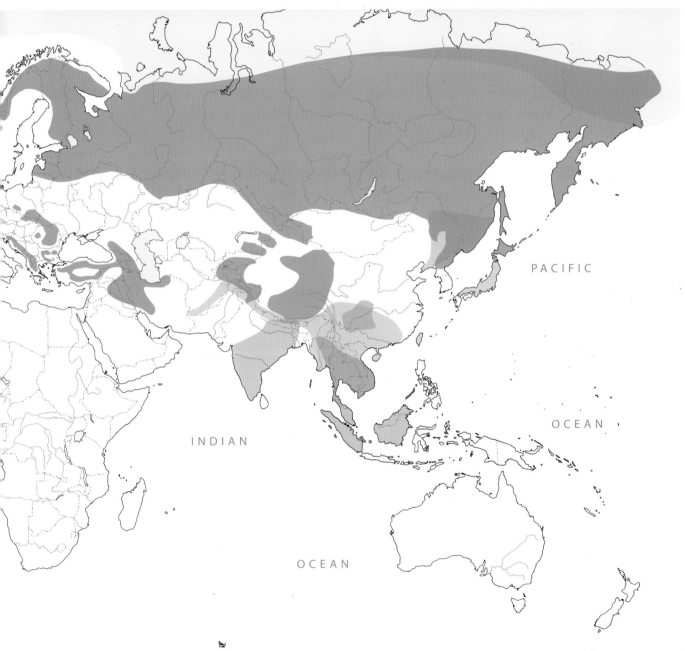

1 The Evolution of Mammals

Bears, like all mammals, are warm-blooded animals, covered with hair, and the females have mammary glands that produce milk to feed their young. Most people are surprised to learn that mammals pre-date even the dinosaurs. Mammal and mammal-like fossils have been found in rocky sediments dating back over 300 million years ago. A competitive race between mammals and reptiles began to take place for world dominance, and one group of reptiles became better suited to the environment at the time and began to flourish. Those successful reptiles would become the animals we now know as the dinosaurs. They would be the dominant class of animal life on Earth for the next 250 million years. Mammals and all other land animals were reduced to minor roles in the ecology of the time.

During the long reign of these wondrous and successful creatures, mammals continued slowly to evolve. We know very little about them, however, as few fossil records have been found for this period of time. The few scattered clues that paleontologists have uncovered suggest that they were small, rat-sized animals that likely sought safety from dinosaurian and other reptilian predators in the underbrush and forests. Even these few remains, however, suggest that placental, marsupial, and herbivorous traits were developing in mammals way back then.

During the reign of the dinosaurs mammals were small and kept to the undergrowth. Meat-eating dinosaurs would have preyed on them occasionally. Illustration: Carnosaur.

The dinosaurs died out 65 million years ago. Although the exact reason for the dinosaurs' extinction remains a mystery, there is strong evidence that supports the theory that a 16 kilometre-wide (10 mile) asteroid crashed into Earth near Mexico's Yucatan Peninsula. The impact threw up a massive dust cloud that enveloped Earth and altered the ecosystem to such an extent that only smaller land animals survived. The dinosaurs' disappearance opened the door for other groups of animals to dominate the land.

Two groups in particular fought it out—the birds and the mammals. Both were warm-blooded and covered with insulating coats—feathers or hair. For a time it appeared that the birds would win the battle—some were large enough to prey on animals the size of large dogs! However, mammals proved to have the advantage of giving birth to live young rather than laying eggs. This characteristic allowed the mammals to assume the dominant role within a few million years of the dinosaurs' passing.

Fossil records dating back about 60 million years reveal the first evidence of the mammal group that would eventually become bears and other carnivores. Within a span of just a few million years, the two major lines of the order Carnivora were established. One branch includes the cat-like carnivores. Known as the *viverravines*, it gave rise to modern cats, hyenas, genets, civets, and mongooses. The other branch includes the dog-like carnivores. These are referred to as vulpavine, and this line gave rise to dogs, weasels, raccoons, and bears.

Most predators of that period possessed specialized teeth, designed for killing and tearing apart their prey, but carnivores share a different set of dental characteristics than other meat eaters. The word carnivore has come to mean "meat eater," but it also refers to a distinct group of mammals with carnassial teeth—teeth that are especially adapted to the cutting of flesh. On each side of the jaw, the last upper

Birds evolved from a family of dinosaurs known as "raptors." Like modern birds there is evidence that many species of dinosaurs laid eggs in nests and even fed their hatchlings there. Illustrated: Oviraptor

premolar and the first lower molar have been modified to perform like scissors. They cut or shear meat from the bone. If you've ever watched a cat or dog chewing on a bone you have seen these specialized teeth in action. All members of the order Carnivora have these teeth or (in the case of some bears) had direct ancestors that possessed them.

○ Birds are now widely believed to be a branch of the dinosaur family, descended from a family of predatory dinosaurs known as raptors.

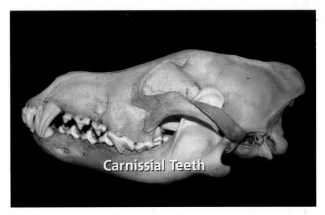

This wolf skull illustrates the typical carnissial teeth found in most members of the Order Carnivora. They are clearly designed for shearing.

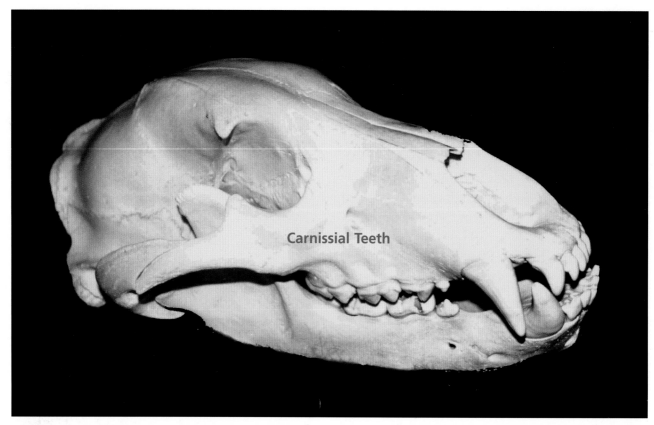

Carnissial Teeth

Forty million years ago a group of small carnivorous mammals began to develop the traits that would later identify them as the ancestors of the animals we now call bears. They were small predators, not much larger than today's foxes.

While the true carnivores were developing, the dominant meat eaters on land were likely birds, marsupials, and creodonts (meat-eating mammals that resembled true carnivores but lacked carnassial teeth). Some marsupials developed saber-like teeth and some creodonts grew to the size of today's bears. Even some ungulates (mammals with hooves) gave it a try, though today, most ungulates, such as deer, giraffe, and bison, are plant eaters. An exception is the modern pig, both wild and domestic, that will readily eat meat if offered on the menu.

It was within this competition for prey, 20 to 30 million years ago, that the bear family began to develop along with the other carnivores. Creodonts were the dominant meat eaters until the carnivores displaced them. Two factors likely led to this successful overthrow. First, 30 million years ago Earth was experiencing a cooling trend that reduced the amount of plants available for herbivores. This would have reduced the creodonts' supply of prey. Second, carnivores had a more diversified set of teeth than the other predators and could also feed on plants. Creodonts were, it appears, meat eaters only. The carnivores ability to be omnivores may have tipped the balance in their favour. By 10 million years ago, the creodonts were extinct.

Black Bear Classification

Kingdom	Animalia (animals)
Phylum	Chordata (animals with backbones)
Class	Mammalia (mammals)
Order	Carnivora (carnivores)
Family	Ursidae (bears)
Genus	*Ursus* (bears)
Species	*Americanus* (black bears)

Black Bear Family Tree

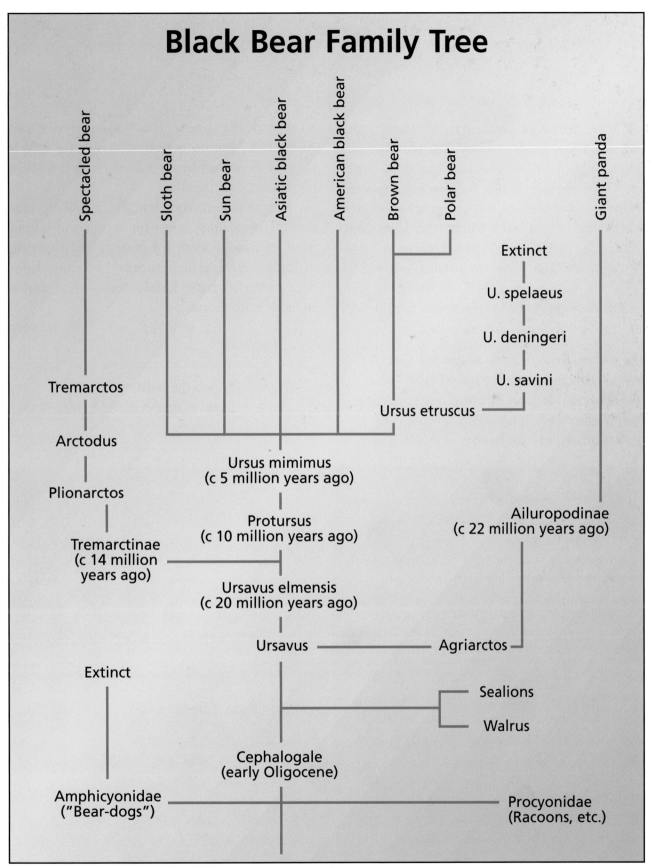

A brief evolutionary history of bears.

2 The Carnivores

There are seven families of carnivores living on Earth today. They include the cats (puma, lion, leopard, cheetah), the dogs (wolf, fox, wild dog, jackal), the hyenas (spotted hyena, brown hyena,) the civets (civet, genet, mongoose), the weasels (otter, skunk, marten, fisher), the raccoons (red panda, raccoon, coatimundi), and the bears. In total, there are 93 different genera and 231 different species found in this group. Of the seven families, all are native to North America except two: the civet and the hyena families. Australia and Antarctica have no members except for canids (dogs) introduced by man. Only Asia can claim members of all families.

A typical carnivore has the following features: large canine teeth for biting and killing prey; carnassial teeth for cutting and shearing meat; powerful, agile bodies and a strong skeleton; powerful jaws; fused wrist bones; and a reduced collarbone.

The hunting style of carnivores is very

The order Carnivora has seven families:
below & facing page **are members of each: African lion, raccoon, spotted genet, spotted hyena,** *overleaf:* **long-tailed weasel, grey wolf, and black bear.**

○ The African lion, the Indian tiger, and the grey wolf are classic examples of the popular image of today's carnivores.

Hyenas were once believed to be cowardly scavengers but in fact they are excellent hunters. This one is carrying off the remains of a Thompson's gazelle that it killed. The sight of such killing repulses many people, but in nature there are no bad or good animals.

The red fox is the most widespread of the carnivores.

diverse. Some, like the wolf, the hyena, and the wild dog, are coursers. That is, they chase down their prey. These animals have large lungs and are able to run long distances. This hunting style developed to allow smaller predators to bring down prey larger than themselves. A single wolf can hardly hope to kill an adult moose, but a pack of wolves can. While one animal distracts the exhausted victim, others rush in and attack. Gradually, the prey is weakened by blood loss and no longer able to fend off its enemies. The exhausted prey is often eaten while still alive. This trait has not endeared them to people who find this method of killing repulsive, and is one of the reasons these animals are widely hunted.

Other carnivores developed lifestyles that were more solitary. Although it was harder to take down larger animals, they didn't need to share their prey. Cats are a good example of this. Most cats hunt by stalking their prey and then making a short charge to capture it. Death is usually quick, either through strangulation or a bite to the head. Cats have given up the powerful lungs of the dogs and hyenas in favour of the sleek, narrow-chested bodies of the short-distance sprinter. Tigers, leopards, and even the house cat practice this type of hunting.

Though some carnivores, like the bears, are large, most are smaller than a German shepherd. The most successful and widespread, however, are some of the smaller species. The red fox is the most widespread of all of the living carnivores and is found on every continent but Antarctica, although it was introduced to Australia and parts of Africa by British gentry intent on having their fox hunt. They thrive in urban areas in Europe and North America. Great numbers of mongooses are found in heavily populated India. Raccoons have invaded most large eastern North American cities, living in chimneys and garages.

On the other hand, some of the rarest and most endangered animals in the world are carnivores. Among these are the black-footed ferret of North America and the giant panda of China.

Why did the carnivores succeed where other predators failed? It was most likely due to a combination of characteristics: specialized teeth, greater intelligence, and an ability to adapt to changing climates and environments.

The black-footed ferret is one of the most endangered species of carnivores. This one photographed at the Metro Toronto Zoo is part of a captive breeding program to restore these animals to the wild.

3 Bears As Omnivores

The bear family has the distinction of having the largest living carnivore—the polar bear—and the largest plant-eating carnivore—the giant panda bear. This family also lays claim to the largest carnivorous mammal ever to walk on Earth—the giant short-faced bear (*Arctodus simus*).

How did such a great diversity of bears evolve? While other carnivores became specialists in their food preferences, the bears kept their options open by becoming omnivorous. While all carnivores eat some plant material as well as meat, only the bear family actively pursued a diet that contained large amounts of vegetation. Even today, when their preferred food of seals is in short supply, the polar bear will munch on seaweed and berries when available.

The preference for a more generalized diet strongly affected the evolution of bears. Where other carnivores (the weasels and mongooses) remained small and sleek in order to pursue their prey in the underbrush, up trees, or underground, the bears grew larger. Where many of the larger carnivores (saber-tooth cats, dire wolves, lions, hyenas, and hunting dogs) adapted to walk on their toes so that they might better chase their prey, bears walked on the soles of their feet, content to amble along in pursuit of whatever came their way, plant or animal.

In the process of becoming a plant eater, the bear's carnassial teeth flattened out. The upper carnassials became smaller and more molar-like. The lower carnassials, the shearing cusps, became flatter and blunter so they presented a better surface for crushing the pulpy surface of plants. By 25 million years ago, this process, called hypocarnivory (the change from carnivore to omnivore) was largely completed.

Although the fossil record for bears can be

The bear family has the distinction of having the largest living carnivore—the polar bear—and the largest plant-eating carnivore (omnivore)— the giant panda bear.

traced back nearly 40 million years, it was not until 10 million years ago that the bear emerged as a major player in the ecosystem. At that time changing climatic patterns, particularly in the northern hemisphere, created the sort of food patterns bears were best able to take advantage of. Seasonal abundance of plants, fish, and animals suited the bears just fine. If one food vanished, then the bears would simply switch to another. If, as happens in winter, no food was available the bear family alone among the carnivores found the perfect solution. They just slept the barren season away, living on stored fat.

Once conditions were right, the bears exploded on the scene and, within a few million years, there were several varieties walking Earth. Although most remained generalists, a few developed a more limited palette, a trend that continues to this day: the giant panda is almost entirely a plant eater, and the polar bear is, in most of its range, entirely a meat eater.

This brown-phase black bear is feeding on dandelions, which it clearly relished.

4 The Giant Short-faced Bear

Two species of short-faced bears roamed the continent during the Quaternary period 2 million to 10,000 years ago. For 500,000 of these years, black bears shared North America with its giant cousins, sometimes called "bulldog bears" because of their unusually short muzzles. The larger of the two species was the giant short-faced bear (*Arctodus simus*).

It was a time when the fauna of North America rivaled that of today's African Serengeti. Among the animals present were elephants, saber-toothed cats, giant sloths, mammoths and mastodons, American lions and cheetahs, dire wolves, giant bison, musk ox, relatives of moose, and bears. The giant short-faced bear was the largest carnivore of the time, terrorizing and feeding on most of these species. Its presence on the Alaskan steppe is credited with keeping the invasion of the much smaller brown (grizzly) bears from Asia at bay.

Some researchers believe they also preyed on black bears, discouraging them from exploiting the open plains and tundra. The black bear likely confined themselves mainly to forested habitats to avoid being on the dinner menu of their larger, more aggressive relatives, as well as the other large predators.

When standing on its hind legs, the great short-faced bear reached as tall as 3.4 metres (11 feet).

The biggest specimens found so far would have been nearly 1.5 metres (5 feet) at the shoulder when walking normally. When standing on its hind legs, it would have been 3.4 metres tall (11 feet). Giant short-faced bears were taller than brown bears but not as heavily built. It is estimated that their autumn weight would have approached 700 kilograms (1,540 pounds). By comparison, today's Kodiak brown bear, the giant of the species, weighs between 635 and 725 kilograms (1,400 and 1,600 pounds). The largest specimen of *A. simus* would have weighed an estimated 1,000 kilograms (2,200 pounds), females being 25 percent smaller.

There is no doubt that the giant short-faced bear was a meat eater. Its carnassial teeth were well developed for shearing, and it had large conical canine teeth resembling those found in large cats. A study of fossil bones by Paul Matheus of the University of Alaska Museum

The giant short-faced bear became extinct only 11,000 years ago and was North America's largest predator at the time.

This reconstruction of the giant short-faced bear shows it walking by a herd of bison, one of its prey sources.

in Fairbanks revealed distinctive wear patterns on the teeth, indicating that the giant short-faced bear did not eat much vegetation.

Matheus believes, however, that the bear was not a hunter, but a scavenger, living off the kills of dire wolves, saber-toothed cats, and American lions. He bases this conclusion on three features. First, the bear's jaws were most powerful when only half open, a better design for crushing bones and extracting marrow than biting prey. Second, a well developed pelvic area suggests a lot of time standing on the back legs, a stance ideally suited to intimidating competitors at a carcass. Third, the short nose and wide nostrils, typical of animals that use smell to locate food, would have allowed the bear to sniff out the remains of a kill.

On the other hand, its long legs would have given the bear the speed needed to run down prey. In fact, its feet differed from others bears in an important way. While today's bears are pigeon-toed, with in-turning front feet, the giant short-faced bear's paws pointed forward—ideal for chasing down prey.

The features that Matheus views as supporting a scavenger could just as well support the characteristics of a predator. Perhaps the bear stood to deliver a powerful, fatal blow. Perhaps the powerful jaws were used to kill its prey. Perhaps it used its keen sense of smell to find prey hidden over the next hill.

It seems most likely that, like today's hyena, the bear was an opportunist—killing when it could, scavenging if at all possible. This description fits most of today's large predators, from polar bears to lions.

The giant short-faced bear became extinct at the same time as the disappearance of the rest of North America's megafauna. It appears to have survived longest in the southern portion of its range, disappearing from Alaska and the Yukon first. The last fossil record for this species dates from about 12,000 years ago. But what killed it off?

It is interesting to note that the species that did survive past the arrival of humans all share one common feature—they are all generalists. That is, their diet was not tied to any one species, plant or animal. This gives us a clue to the disappearance of the giant short-faced bear and its prey. Changing climates brought on by the end of the ice age may have changed the vegetation available to the large herbivores. Unable to find enough food, they died out, taking with them their major predators: lions, American cheetahs, dire wolves, and the short-faced bear.

On the other hand, new research suggests that the heyday of North American megafauna was several thousand years before the end of the last ice age. By 20,000 years ago numbers were already in decline.

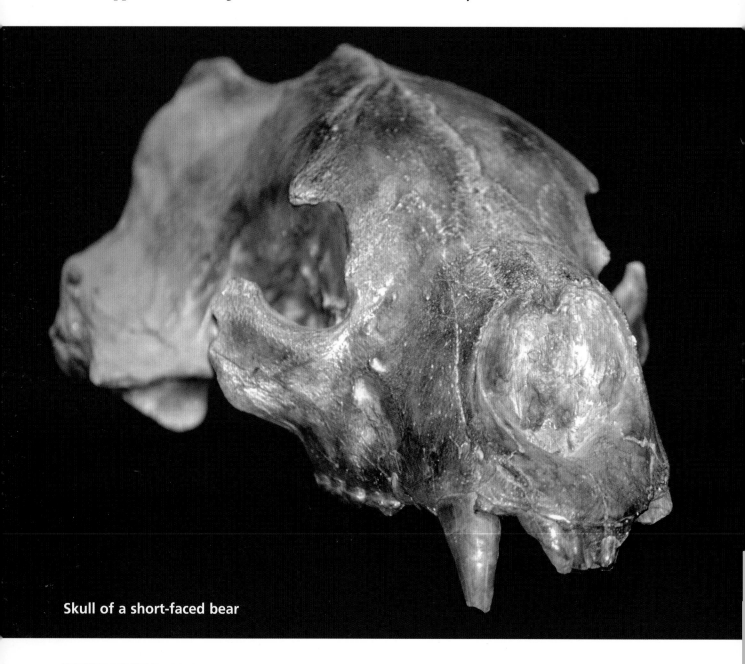

Skull of a short-faced bear

Another compelling theory is that the arrival of humans on the continent spelled doom for the short-faced bears, the giant bison, the giant ground sloth, and the mammoths. There is direct proof that humans hunted North America's giant herbivores. A 12,000-year-old Clovis spear tip was found imbedded in a mastodon's skeleton. But to what extent did primitive hunting pressure eliminate the bear's prey species?

There is now a new theory supported by growing evidence that humans invaded North America at least 30,000, and perhaps as early as 40,000, years ago. Did the demise of the giant herbivores take that long to occur, or did the disappearance of many of the species relate to climatic change? Hunting pressure from humans probably served only to finish off the weakened population.

It is with the disappearance of these larger species 14,000 to 8,000 years ago that we find the flourishing of wildlife better able to adapt to living with their human neighbours. Siberian species had been exposed to hunting by humans and had adapted well. In North America, grizzly bears spread rapidly in the habitat once occupied by the giant short-faced bears. As the continental glacier retreated, the grizzly found new homes. From Texas to Alaska and across the tundra as far as Ontario and Quebec, they became the largest predator. The grizzly had two major advantages over the vanished giants. Like the black bear, it was not totally dependent on meat, surviving very nicely on a diet made up of 80 percent vegetation.

And, like the black bear, it could hibernate, escaping those periods when there was no food available.

In the end, it was likely a lack of prey brought about by changing climates that doomed North America's megafauna. Today we can only imagine the world that once existed here and the great bears that dominated much of it.

The giant short-faced bear became extinct at the same time as the disappearance of the rest of North America's megafauna.

There is however, a living trace of this great short-faced bear. A small bear, the spectacled bear (*Tremarctos ornatus*) lives in the forested mountains of Venezuela, Colombia, and down into Bolivia. It climbs trees, feeds mainly on fruit, and looks more like a black bear than anything else. But a close look at its face reveals that it is not evolved from either the grizzly's or the black bear's line (see page 2). The spectacled bear has a very short muzzle and is the only surviving member of the short-faced clan.

5 The Black Bear During and After the Ice Age

Our look back in time at the bears of the past will be completed once we look at what happened to the black bear during the ice age. We know where it was not living—on the ice fields and the open plains, thanks to the giant short-faced bear and other large predators of the American grasslands. The black bear was confined to the forests. As those forests expanded and contracted, so too did the bear's range. In what is now Canada, the land was almost completely covered by ice. The black bear was confined to forested areas in what is now the United States and Mexico, including the areas around the western mountains, the swamps of the Gulf and Florida coasts, the Appalachians, and the Eastern Coast. Imagine the forested areas of this period shaped like a giant horseshoe, with one end in New England, then sweeping down the Appalachians and across the Gulf, then up the Rockies.

It was during this period that many of today's subspecies of black bear acquired their particular characteristics. Species develop in isolation due to the locations of the ice age glaciers. The changing climate created refuges that kept the bears confined and from breeding with black bears from other areas. Today most black bears belong to one subspecies: *Ursus americanus americanus*.

The richest area for black bear subspecies is British Columbia. The sea level dropped by two hundred metres (over 600 feet) as vast amounts of water were held in the glaciers. These lower sea levels exposed land along the coast of Alaska and British Columbia, where black bear populations were isolated. These pockets of bears developed their own specific characteristics (See Chapter 6). As the ice melted, the bears recolonized the interior, although one or two populations remained isolated on

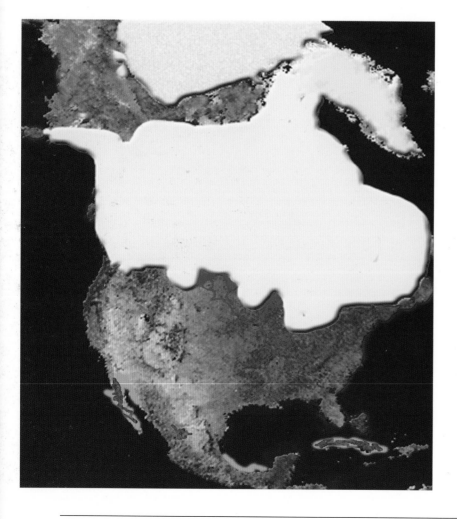

Twenty thousand years ago virtually all of Canada was covered with ice.

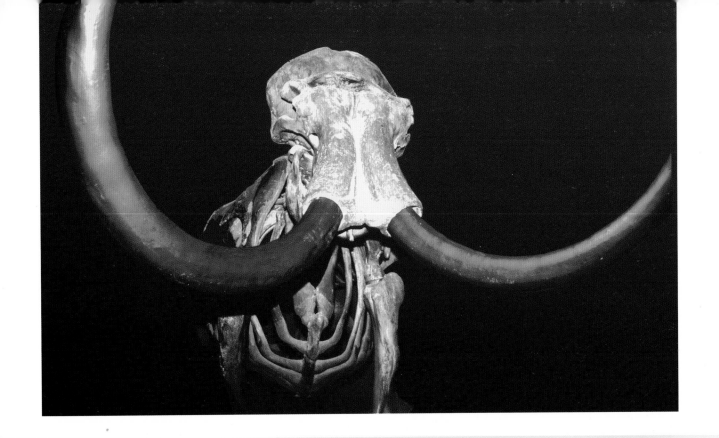

Black bears shared the land with mammoths (skull above), mastodons (reconstructed), and other megafauna, but these other species became extinct by the end of the ice age.

islands such as the Queen Charlottes and Vancouver Island.

Jaguars, mastodons, a giant form of peccary, deer, and an extinct form of moose shared these forests. Giant beaver, as well as the more familiar beaver, were also part of the forest ecosystem, as were wolves and mountain lions.

As the ice retreated, the forest expanded to the north, and so too did the black bear's range. The extinction of the giant short-faced bear did not expose new areas for the black bear—the grizzly quickly filled this vacant range 12,000 years ago, and the black bear could not have competed with their larger, more aggressive cousins.

Black bears may have helped check grizzly bear expansion into much of the newly forested areas of North America. A study conducted by David Mattson (U.S. Geological Survey) and Stephen Herrero (University of Calgary)

hypothesize that black bears out-competed grizzlies in areas where there were relatively low densities of berries and other foods. Boreal and deciduous forests are exactly such places, and grizzlies are not generally associated with these habitats. What was the black bear's advantage? It is smaller and therefore able to exist on lesser amounts of food.

At the same time, another omnivore was inhabiting the coastal land. It is now widely believed that human beings from Asia accessed the North American continent along the exposed west coastal lands of British Columbia and Alaska. Although it is widely accepted that by 14,000 years ago, humans were well established in the area that is now the United States, there is a growing body of evidence that suggests humans have made North and South America their home for at least 30,000 years.

Black bear range

There is a growing body of evidence that suggests humans have made North and South America their home for at least 30,000 years.

As black bears expanded their range into the north with the retreating ice, humans were also occupying these lands. Again, the forest provided a safer habitat that allowed black bears to avoid these new predators. But, increasingly, the early North Americans were being forced to change from a life of hunting big game on the open plains to one that was based on gathering (and eventually growing) plant food. Increased competition for resources would have forced humans into the forest.

Here they would encounter and learn to rely on the black bear. In fact, it was likely that the trails they followed into the woods were made by these bears, who then became a source of meat, fat, and hides. Surviving bears would have quickly learned to avoid humans—they had learned to avoid confrontation throughout their entire existence.

○ Having learned over eons to avoid danger, black bears survived the eventual arrival of the Europeans. Wolves and grizzlies did not fare so well against the arrival of guns and poison that accompanied cattle and sheep ranching.

Woolly mammoth with musk ox

6 The Subspecies of Black Bear

There are 16 subspecies of black bear in North America with British Columbia boasting the most with six. To the average viewer, one black bear pretty much looks like another, unless there are colour differences. Colour, however, is not a very accurate way of determining whether a black bear belongs to one subspecies or another. See chapter 10 for a discussion of colour phases.

A species is any living thing that produces fertile offspring. All black bears can mate and produce offspring capable of having healthy babies, regardless of the subspecies. A black bear could not mate with a polar bear and produce fertile young. Therefore they are different species.

A subspecies displays distinctive features that set it apart from other subspecies. In the past these features were often physical in nature: a larger skull, bigger teeth, or a distinct raised sagittal crest on the skull. Because species and subspecies were sometimes assigned on the basis of very few specimens, the number of recognized species and subspecies changes over time as more specimens are collected and analyzed. The 16 subspecies of black bears identified below reflect current accepted taxonomy, but that number may change with further DNA analysis.

How do species and subspecies evolve? One word sums it up: isolation. In the case of black bears, the various subspecies are believed to have evolved because they became separated from other black bears. The most likely cause of this separation was the continental ice sheet that isolated a number of bear populations geographically, especially in British Columbia and Alaska. These populations survived on islands

Most black bears belong to the subspecies _Ursus americanus americanus_. This was the subspecies first encountered by European naturalists in the 1600's and it became the "type" species. All other subspecies of black bear are compared to the characteristics of this subspecies.

or in coastal valleys where glaciers forced them to retreat.

Elsewhere, expanding and contracting forests that resulted from climate change as the glaciers melted and expanded caused black bears to become isolated, especially in the high country that dots the American prairie. (The Black Hills are a good example.) In other places, natural barriers such as water bodies (Newfoundland) or mountains and deserts (California) isolated populations.

In Ontario, recent research has determined that a population of between 250 and 400 black bears living on the Bruce Pennisula is geneti-cally different from other Ontario and Michigan bears. This population, thought to be the only viable bear population in southwestern Ontario, is not considered a subspecies, but in the hundred or so years since it was isolated, there has been time for it to begin the first steps toward that status.

The population, once isolated, begins to develop small changes in DNA and physical characteristics that allow scientists to determine whether or not it is a true subspecies. The currently accepted subspecies (with their respective ranges) are outlined on the next page.

Subspecies and Status	Range
Ursus americanus altifrontalis	The Pacific northwest coast from central British Columbia through northern California and inland to the tip of northern Idaho and British Columbia. In B.C. this is a coastal sub-species ranging from Oregon to Bella Coola, western Tweedsmuir Provincial Park east into Manning Provincial Park and Lillooet. Primarily black-phase bears.
Ursus americanus amblyceps	Colorado, New Mexico, west Texas, eastern half of Arizona into northern Mexico, southeastern Utah
Ursus americanus americanus This is the most common subspecies (threatened in Mississippi)	From eastern Montana to the Atlantic, from Alaska south and east through Canada to the Atlantic and south to Texas
Ursus americanus californiensis	The Central Valley of California north through southern Oregon
Ursus americanus carlottae	Alaska and in British Columbia an insular subspecies restricted to the Queen Charlottes; massive skull, large molars. Only black phase.
Ursus americanus cinnamomum	Idaho, western Montana, Wyoming; eastern Washington and Oregon, northeastern Utah, most of British Columbia east of the Coast Range. Brown phase is common.
Ursus americanus emmonsii Blue Bear, Glacier Bear	Southeastern Alaska, northeast and extreme northwest of British Columbia, primarily in Tatshenshini Provincial Park and adjacent Alaska
Ursus americanus eremicus Mexican Black Bear (threatened)	Northeastern Mexico, southeastern Texas
Ursus americanus floridanus Florida Black Bear (threatened)	Florida, southern Georgia, Alabama
Ursus americanus hamiltoni	The island of Newfoundland
Ursus americanus kermodei Kermode's Black Bear, White Bear	Restricted to the coastal mainland of British Columbia from Burke Channel to the Nass River and most adjacent islands. Includes white and black phases. White phase is most common on Princess Royal and Gribbel Islands (about 10% of bears) but is seen occasionally throughout the range.
Ursus americanus luteolus Louisiana Black Bear (threatened)	Eastern Texas, Louisiana, southern Mississippi
Ursus americanus machetes	North-central Mexico
Ursus americanus perniger	Kenai Peninsula, Alaska
Ursus americanus pugnax	Alexander Archipelago, Alaska
Ursus americanus vancouveri	Insular race restricted to Vancouver Island and larger adjacent islands; large like *U. a. carlottae* but has smaller teeth. Primarily black-phase

Part II: The Black Bear's World

7 Adaptations for Forest Life

It is rare to see a black bear in the woods because it chooses not to show itself. On those rare occasions when one is spotted during a hike, it is usually near a stream. Presumably, the noise of the water masks the hiker's approach. Invariably, no matter how close humans get to it, the bear will retreat at a run into the woods. However, bears certainly have been known to actually seek out people for the opportunity to beg for or steal food. These habituated bears are quite another matter, and their behaviour is atypical of a wilderness black bear.

The forest provides a safe haven for the black bear. It subscribes to the philosophy that the better part of valour is retreat. Unlike the grizzly bear, which takes an aggressive stance and charges, a quick turn off the trail and the black bear is gone. The black coat, which is the most common colour phase of the species in the east, blends in well with forest shadows; it is an effective means of camouflage. Hiding places are abundant in the forest, both on the ground and, in a pinch, in the treetops.

Black bears are often sighted near streams, where the noise of the water masks a visitor's approach.

The bear's dark colour provides good camouflage in the forest shadows.

The black bear has curved claws it uses for climbing trees to seek food or to escape enemies. Female bears will send their cubs up a tree and leave them there until they feel it is safe for the cubs to come down. It has been suggested that as a bear gets bigger, its climbing ability lessens. That may be so, but all black bears can climb trees—even the big males. Contrary to the popular notion, you cannot escape a black bear by climbing a tree.

The bears' curved claws allow them to climb straight up a tree trunk.

Above A mother and two yearling cubs rest in safety during the mid-day heat. Sows will even feed their cubs in trees.

Bear cubs learn quickly how to climb trees to avoid danger.

Right Taking a break from snacking, or just hanging out? Larger bears are less likely to climb a tree for a nap, but food is another matter.

This is a bear nest. A black bear fed in this beech tree and, as it did, it broke off branches and stuffed them underneath its bottom.
The damage to the tree was significant.

Damage to trees can be substantial when the fall mast of acorns or beechnuts ripen. Adult bears will clamber up into the treetops in search of food, breaking off branches as they go. Bears climb trees by grasping hold of the trunk with their front paws and then walking up the tree with their back paws. This results in a curious, inchworm-like action as they go up or down. Unlike squirrels, for example, bears cannot go down a tree headfirst.

Being forest dwellers, these bears rely more on their sense of smell than their sense of sight. They follow their noses, using it to sniff out food, test the air for danger, and locate a mate. This sense is so well developed that they can detect the slight scent of a hidden fawn, a distant moose calf, or even human garbage buried under 30 centimetres (one foot) of soil. In the forest, where food is likely to be localized at different times of the year, this ability is very important.

For a northern forest dweller, the ability to find enough food is a crucial skill. Even with its diverse feeding habits, there is just barely enough food to go around. Here, again, the bear has adapted well, for it is a loner by nature. Two or more bears will not stay together for long unless they are courting or they are female and young. This tendency to prefer a solitary lifestyle is a typical adaptation of all forest animals. The forest's bounty tends to be scattered both in season and location. Fawns are available in the spring, as are spring flowers. Berries ripen in August. Acorns can be harvested in the fall. All of these food sources are likely to be spread over a considerable area and exist only in patches, so the less it has to share that food with other bears, the better.

Perhaps the black bear's best adaptation to forest life, however, is its ability to hibernate throughout the winter months when there is no food available. Chapters 12, 13, and 14 deal with this fascinating process.

A log ripped by a bear in search of insects and grubs.

A black bear also uses its claws to rip apart rotten logs to get at the insect grubs that live there. Unlike the grizzly, black bears are lazier and seldom bother to dig for food.

Bears rely heavily on their sense of smell to find food, avoid danger, and find a mate.

8 Black Bear Habitat

The ideal habitat for black bears is a place that provides food, shelter, and water in ample supply for them to grow large, have healthy litters, and for there to be sufficient numbers for breeding. The availability of enough food is obviously paramount. One of the best areas for producing just such a bear population is Riding Mountain National Park in Manitoba. The black bear population is quite healthy, and the park boasts some of the largest black bears on the continent. There are 0.1 to 1.3 black bears per square kilometre (0.3 to 3.4 per square mile), depending on the quality of their habitat. Although this density lies only in the middle range of North America's black bears, there are other factors at play here. Farms and ranches surround the park, and wandering bears are often poached or shot. The loss of these animals from the population accounts for the reported "average" number of animals.

A better way of assessing the habitat quality is to look at the bear's reproductive success. Riding Mountain's bears breed earlier and have more cubs than most other bear populations. One female had five cubs at least three times

during the period the bears were being studied. Although she never succeeded in keeping all five alive through their first season, most of her cubs did survive. The average number of cubs here lies between two and three per litter.

Ample food is obviously required, and the forest is the main source in the fall, when the acorns and berry crops ripen, but open grasslands, marshes, and meadows also provide nourishment in the spring when the rich young ground plants begin to flourish. Riding Mountain has a mixture of clearings, lakes, and deciduous forests, all of which are utilized by the resident bears. These glades and forests also provide other sources of food in the form of elk calves and whitetail fawns in the spring, and there is an abundant supply of insects in summer. Such a habitat provides a variety of foods throughout the active time of the bear's year.

Aside from abundant food, black bears require sufficient cover to escape from resident enemies. In the remote, treeless tundra regions of Labrador, some black bears are able to survive because of the absence of their two major predators: grizzly bears and humans. These tundra bears have a much lower reproductive rate and occupy much larger territories than do the forest-dwelling blacks.

In the west, in areas where black bears do not fall prey to grizzlies or humans, they will feed part of the time on open hillsides, far from the nearest forest. On the other hand, where predators are active, as in the eastern half of the continent, the bear becomes a true forest animal.

Black bear habitat must have sufficient cover for bears to hide in, open areas such as

Classic black bear habitat, Riding Mountain National Park, Manitoba.

Alaska's and British Columbia's glaciers are receding, creating new bear habitat.

meadows, marshes or glades to graze in and lots of room. Water is also important. How these factors combine varies. Nevertheless black bears can be found in some of the most scenic parts of North America.

How much area is required for a viable breeding population to exist? Studies conducted in southern Canada and the northeastern United States, where much of the forest cover is gone, suggest that black bears need a minimum of 4,050 hectares (10,000 acres) of uninterrupted forest cover to survive in richer habitats, and 10,120 hectares (25,000 acres) in poorer ones. Recent studies have found that where bears are not heavily poached or hunted, they can live in smaller areas.

Are there other factors that limit black bear numbers? A study done of black bears living on Stockton Island in Lake Superior sheds some light. At the beginning of the study there were 3 bears living on the 40.7 square kilometre

(15.7 square mile) island. Three years later there were 20, not counting cubs, or more than 0.4 bears per square kilometre (1 per square mile). This was almost double the average density in North America (0.24 bears per square kilometre or 0.65 per square mile).

Two years later, one case of death by starvation and five cases of cannibalism were recorded. The females in the population entered their first breeding season one or two years later than bears on the mainland, first year cub size declined, and cub mortality increased, all serving to further reduce population growth

This study suggests that black bears, left to their own, will regulate their numbers, but the exact mechanisms at work still require more study. The problem in studying these populations is that there are very few places in North America where black bear numbers are not affected by such activities as hunting, poaching, and road accidents.

A combination of meadows, glades, forest, and water provide an ideal habitat.

Left Many black bears make Algonquin Provincial Park in Ontario their home.

Above Yosemite National Park in California has a large black bear population.

Below Temperate rain forest, British Columbia.

9 Physical Characteristics

Most people overestimate the size of wild animals. They are surprised when they see the animals in zoos or museums, and often comment that they thought they were much bigger. The more dangerous the animal, the bigger it is perceived to be, especially if it is a bear that you encounter while out for a hike in the woods.

Most black bears weigh about the same as an average human male. Typically, they will fall between 80 and 100 kilograms (between 160 and 220 pounds). A good-sized black bear approaches 125 kilograms (250 pounds), and a few can even reach close to 250 kilograms (500 pounds). Male black bears reach their maxi-

mum height and length when they are seven or eight years old. The biggest black bear ever recorded in Ontario weighed 345 kilograms (760 pounds) and measured over two metres (two yards) long. A tractor-trailer struck and killed it on a highway. The heaviest on record weighed 364 kilograms (803 pounds). It was shot in Manitoba. As a general rule, the biggest black bears come from the northeastern states and the eastern provinces.

Males tend to be one-third larger than females, but there is such a variety in size that you cannot reliably identify the sex of a bear by size alone.

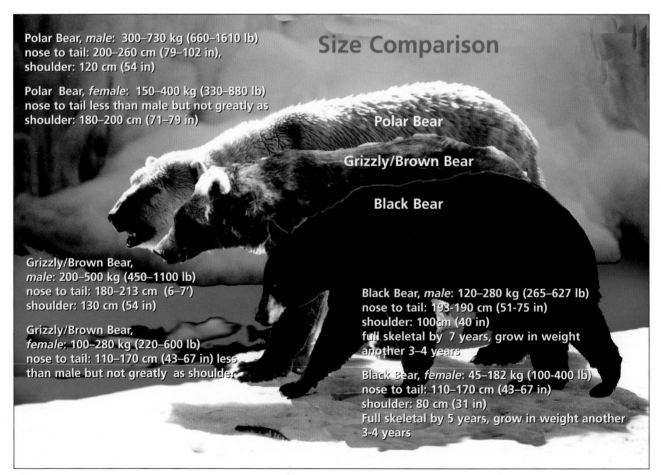

Size Comparison

Polar Bear, *male*: 300–730 kg (660–1610 lb)
nose to tail: 200–260 cm (79–102 in),
shoulder: 120 cm (54 in)

Polar Bear, *female*: 150–400 kg (330–880 lb)
nose to tail less than male but not greatly as
shoulder: 180–200 cm (71–79 in)

Polar Bear

Grizzly/Brown Bear

Black Bear

Grizzly/Brown Bear,
male: 200–500 kg (450–1100 lb)
nose to tail: 180–213 cm (6–7')
shoulder: 130 cm (54 in)

Grizzly/Brown Bear,
female: 100–280 kg (220–600 lb)
nose to tail: 110–170 cm (43–67 in) less
than male but not greatly as shoulder

Black Bear, *male*: 120–280 kg (265–627 lb)
nose to tail: 193-190 cm (51-75 in)
shoulder: 100cm (40 in)
full skeletal by 7 years, grow in weight
another 3-4 years

Black Bear, *female*: 45–182 kg (100-400 lb)
nose to tail: 110–170 cm (43–67 in)
shoulder: 80 cm (31 in)
Full skeletal by 5 years, grow in weight another
3-4 years

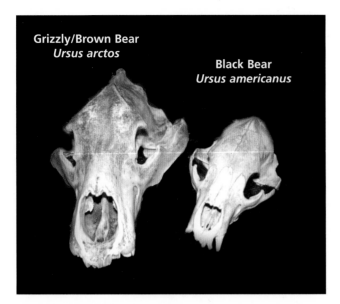

Grizzly/Brown Bear
Ursus arctos

Black Bear
Ursus americanus

These skulls illustrate the difference in size between the grizzly and the black bear.

Size alone is also not an especially good way of distinguishing a brown-coloured black bear from a grizzly bear. A large black bear can be bigger than a small or even average grizzly. A better way of telling is to look at the body shape. Black bears have a "droopy" backside that makes their back legs appear much shorter than their front legs. A grizzly has a much straighter back and a characteristic shoulder hump, which black bears lack. A grizzly bear's head has a dish-shaped (concave) profile while a black bear's head is straighter. Black bear claws are shorter than the grizzly's. They range from 2.5 to 3.5 centimetres (1 to 1.4 inches), where a grizzly's are 5 to 7 centimetres (2 to 2.8 inches) long.

You can tell brown-coloured black bears and grizzlies apart sometimes by their size, but more reliably by their shape. Note the characteristic shoulder hump of the grizzly (below) and the droopy backside and straighter head profile of the black bear (over, bottom).

You can judge a bear's age by its ears. The larger the ears appear relative to the size of the head, the younger the bear. This cub-of-the-year appears to have large ears in relation to its head size.

The ears still appear to be large on this three- to four-year-old male, who likely weighs about 75 kilograms (140 pounds).

A broad head and large neck are typical of adult males.

All bears have an excellent sense of smell, which is the primary means of locating food, and, contrary to popular belief, they can also see very well. One bear was observed reacting to another well over a kilometre (about a mile) away. The wind was blowing away from the intruder, so it was clear that eyesight alone was responsible for detecting the other bear. Because they are forest animals, though, they have a limited need to see great distances. Bears also hear very well.

Black bears are covered with a thick coat of hair—actually, two types of hair. They have a soft, dense under-fur for insulation, and long, coarse guard hairs that overlap and keep the under-fur clean and dry. Each spring the bears shed their winter coats, and they can look quite straggly. By summer, though, the new coat is well established.

Black bears also have a musky smell about them that can be quite noticeable when you are in close range.

The average life span for adult bears is 18 years, and if all goes well, a black bear can live into its twenties. The oldest ever observed in the wild was 31, while the oldest in a zoo lived to be 44. Reaching such an advanced age is rare, just as reaching 100 is rare for humans.

The average life span for adult bears is 18 years, and if all goes well, a black bear can live into its twenties.

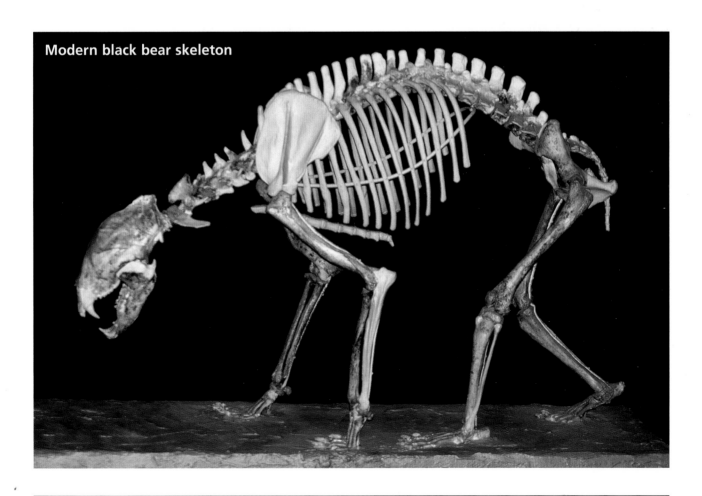

Modern black bear skeleton

10 What Is Black, Brown, White, Blue and Still Black Through and Through?

All the bears pictured on these pages are black bears, even though they are not all black. Of all the world's living carnivores, the black bear has the greatest colour variation. Wolves have the second greatest variation, but not even they can claim blue among their colours.

Why is the black bear so named if not all are black? When settlers arrived in North America, they were already familiar with the brown bears of Europe. By this time, brown bears were noticeably absent from eastern North America, so the bears the settlers encountered were, for the most part, black. The farther west Europeans moved, however, the more variety of colour they came across. Several new species of bear were originally identified, but when it became clear that the cinnamon-coloured bear could give birth to black bear cubs and vice versa, the new species were dropped.

There is no doubt that all of these colour phases belong to the same species. Black bears of one colour routinely have offspring of other colours. Some brown black bears darken with age, further complicating matters.

What caused this great diversity? The best theory has to do with heat regulation. Black-coloured bears favoured the eastern forests because of the shade provided there. Aside from being a good camouflage colour in the dark woods, the black phase provided greater warmth in spring and fall. Researchers have observed that black-coloured bears rarely leave the shaded forest in summer to feed during the day, probably because they would overheat. To cool down, the bears will wade into streams or soak their paws and rub the water onto their heads. Swamps and cool spruce forests lining streams are used to avoid the summer's heat. Reports suggest that they might also return to their dens to cool themselves.

Brown-coloured black bears are found in the west where the forests have more open spaces. Here, they often feed on exposed hillsides during the day while the black-coloured ones keep to the forested areas. Presumably, the lighter shade absorbs less heat and makes the sun's rays more tolerable.

The blue-coloured or glacier bear is found only along the southeastern coast of Alaska. Its bluish cast might be a way of blending in with the glaciers that are found here, but this seems unlikely because there would be little reason for the bear to venture onto a glacier, as there is no food there. The lighter coloured guard hairs, which give the glacier bear its unique appearance, may serve a similar function to that of the polar bear's guard hairs—to bring extra heat to the bear's skin in these cooler climates.

Why, then, are Kermode's bears white? They are found for the most part on remote islands off the coast of British Columbia, in dense temperate rain forests where there are no glaciers and little snow. The white coloration would seem to serve no function at all, yet they are not albinos but true white bears. Albinos have pink eyes and noses, but the Kermode's nose and eyes are the same as all black bears. In fact, it is not unusual for a white cub to have a black sibling.

What is black, brown, blonde, cinnamon, chocolate, white, and blue? Why, the black bear, of course.

All colour phases can produce black cubs, and not all cubs stay the same colour when they grow up. Confusing, isn't it?

○ Though mostly found on remote islands off the coast of British Columbia, white-phase black bears have been seen in other areas of North America. The most recent sighting was at the Vince Shute Wildlife Sanctuary, Minnesota, in the mid-1990s. However, these bears make up less than 1/10ᵗʰ of one percent of the region's population.

Why are they white only on these remote islands and the few places they are found on the mainland? Again, the literature is speculative and suggests a possible tie to the ice age. It is believed that some black bears were isolated by the continental ice fields and developed this colour phase because there were few or no predators to prey on them. Their colour, of course, would attract predators, but isolated on the heavily wooded islands, where few large predators existed, the white colour phase was able to establish itself and continues to this day. There are grizzlies and wolves on these islands, but the island environment is so rich in prey, such as black-tailed deer and salmon, that there is no need to hunt these bears.

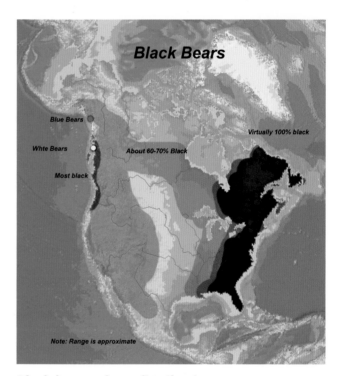

Black bear colour distribution

○ White-coloured (not albino) squirrels, deer, and even a tiger have all been found living among the dominant-coloured species.

11 Events Leading Up to Hibernation

Bears of more southern climates, such as the Asian sun bear and the Asian black bear, live in regions that, even at the height of the ice age, remained relatively mild. Food in some form is also available all year round. These bears, as a general rule, do not hibernate. But for bears living in colder climates, the evolutionary change to becoming an omnivore made it too difficult to survive the winter. They had grown too large and cumbersome to chase prey through the snow. The winter plants that were available for the large ungulates, such as deer, moose, and bison, were too low in nutrients for the bear. Hibernation was the perfect solution.

But how do they do it? What triggers hibernation? Where do they go? What happens to them during the period they are hibernating?

In the late summer and early fall black bears begin gorging themselves on a variety of foods in preparation for their winter sleep. They will consume three times more food per day at this time of year than they do in the spring and early summer (63,000 to 84,0000 kilojoules, or 15,000 to 20,000 kilocalories). Feeding goes on almost 20 hours a day and all other activities stop. This "binging" is called hyperphagia. In the process, they will gain up to one-third of their normal body weight as they build up fat reserves. In one study, bears gained one kilogram (over two pounds) a day during this period, and some bears actually *doubled* their weight before entering hibernation!

This cub-of-the-year looks fat enough to survive until spring.

The bears will consume three times more food per day at this time of year than they do in the spring and early summer.

What starts this binge? The current theory is that it may be related to photoperiodism. The amount of sunlight and its angle triggers certain changes in the chemical makeup of the animal. This mechanism causes deer to grow antlers in the spring and to stop growing them in the fall.

Is the abundance of food in late summer a factor? Berries and acorns ripen and are readily available in good years. However, the mere availability of food does not, in itself, explain a black bear's sudden feeding binge. Even when food is abundant in the spring and early summer, they eat just enough at this time to balance their energy losses.

It is interesting to note that bears cannot "sleep" through a poor summer crop. They will

This meal of hawberry leftovers in Manitoba is likely one of the last of the season.

starve to death, even though three months later they are more than able to enter a dormant state. This fact supports the theory of sunlight as a trigger for the bear's body to enter hibernation.

After this feeding stage, the bear enters a sort of walking hibernation. It is alert, but it eats and drinks very little. Its body systems slowly begin to slow down and blood flow to its limbs gradually decreases.

By now it has chosen and prepared its den site. Some bears will even try out the site for a few days—like testing the bed—disappearing and then reappearing for a few more days of late fall wanderings.

Pregnant sows are the first to den, followed by older sows with cubs, then solitary females, followed by subadults, and finally adult males. They generally emerge from the den in the reverse order, with the largest males appearing first.

Just what triggers the bear's final entry into a den is not clear. It has been suggested that a long snowfall will prompt them, but other factors, such as the shortening of the day and the quality and availability of food, may also prompt them. Or is it that the chemical changes that occur during the period of walking sleep are the major factor? It might just be that for black bears, it's time to go to sleep.

Snow alone is not enough to send bears to their dens.

12 Dens

There is no such thing as a typical den except that it must be dry, located away from danger, and fairly cramped—the more open air around the animal, the more heat it will lose.

A den might be under a brush pile, tree roots, or beneath a rock ledge. Bears have been known to den up in culverts, and some dens have been found under buildings in new subdivisions that have encroached on the bears' range.

This den was dug beneath a spruce tree, and so has many roots hanging down. The tranquilized cub is waiting for its mother to be returned after examination by researchers.

Small caves will be used, but are not as common as the popular notion has us believe. In Ontario's Bruce Peninsula, the retreating glaciers left behind a landscape of limestone rock honeycombed with caves that bears use. Many have vertical drops of about 1.5 metres (5 feet) and then opened into caves that are at least 5 metres long (over 15 feet). Some dens in the area have even greater vertical drops.

Smaller bears often use tree cavities where the tree trunks are at least one metre (one yard) wide. Subadult and female bears are typical users of this type of den. Some have been found over 20 metres (60 feet) up a tree, and there was a den found in Louisiana over 30 metres (100 feet) above ground!

In Tennessee, where there are still large stands of virgin forest, 50 percent of the bears in one study group used tree dens, but in a study conducted in Wisconsin, where there is less old-growth forest, only one bear used a tree den. These bears tended to use non-excavated dens created by windfalls, logging, or thick stands of conifer trees. Some chose just to "nest" on the ground and let the snow cover them.

In the southern United States, brown and black bears will build "nest" surface dens. These are constructed from fallen treetops or branches the bear has bitten through and then piled up.

Bears will build dens in naturally formed cavities created by erosion and deadfalls, but they will also dig their own dens if necessary. For black bears, the typical dug-out den has a short entranceway one to two metres (three to six feet) long. This leads to the sleeping chamber that is egg-shaped and just large enough for

This den in Riding Mountain National Park, Manitoba, has not been used for several years.

Ontario predator biologist Dr. Martyn Obbard is about to hand out a tranquilized cub from this den that is 5 metres (15 feet) long, with a 2 metre (6 foot) drop to the den floor.

The inside of the den.

the bear to twist around in. The sleeping chamber is lined with bedding that is 16 to 22 centimetres (6 to 8 inches) deep and consists of grasses, leaves, mosses, and other forest litter.

How easy is it to find a den? Not very! Den sites are selected for their privacy and security, and once a blanket of snow covers them they are all but invisible. A trained eye might spot likely looking sites, but there are often hundreds of possible locations. There is one telltale feature, though—a breathing hole where the bear's hot breath escapes. It acts like a chimney and exchanges air. At one site, there can be several such holes, but only one is made by the bear's breath. It is easy to spot because frost crystals from the moist, expelled air form at the entrance to the hole.

Often the only sign of a den is a breathing hole.

A black bear is hibernating beneath this little hill.

13 Hibernation

All animals that hibernate do so to escape a period of extremely low food production. They put on fat reserves and select well-insulated dens in which to escape the bone-chilling temperatures of the northern winter. This is true of both bears and those species that are classic hibernators, but it is there that the similarities end.

When a ground squirrel disappears below ground, its temperature and bodily functions fall off rapidly. Its heart rate drops from a normal summertime high of 500 plus beats per minute to 25 or less! Its body metabolism (the rate at which it burns up kilocalories) functions at 1/25th its usual rate, and its body temperature approaches freezing.

○ Ground squirrels, marmots, and groundhogs are all classic hibernators.

A bear's heart rate drops only 8 to 10 beats per minute from its summertime rate of between 40 and 70 beats per minute. Its metabolism continues to function at 50 percent of normal. Thus, in the den, a bear will use about half the food energy it usually does. A bear's body temperature falls only by 3°C to 7°C (5°F to 9°F), and it will die if it drops below 20°C (69° F).

It is virtually impossible to wake a ground squirrel when it is in its hibernating state. A bear, on the other hand, can be roused easily—something to keep in mind should you ever climb into a bear's occupied den! For this reason, bears were, at one time, not considered to be true hibernators.

It is the bear, though, and not the ground squirrel that sleeps the entire winter. Ground squirrels must wake up at regular intervals of between two and six weeks. If they don't, they

> It is virtually impossible to wake a ground squirrel when it is in its hibernating state. A bear, on the other hand, can be roused easily—something to keep in mind should you ever climb into a bear's occupied den!

die! The cost of waking up is very dear. One source estimates that the energy used equals the amount required during 10 days of hibernation. Why do they do it? To visit the bathroom and grab a bite to eat, of course! Since they are unable to reuse their bodily wastes, they must eliminate them or risk poisoning themselves. They must snack on stored food to replace this loss and to maintain their body weight.

Bears, while they do lose weight during hibernation, use up little bone or muscle mass, unlike ground squirrels. A bear's metabolism burns only fat, not carbohydrates or proteins like the other hibernators. The burning of fat produces several by-products, most of which the bear reuses. One by-product is water, which allows the bear to go without drinking during its winter sleep.

Groundhogs hibernate in a deep sleep more similar to that of ground squirrels than bears.

Urine production is low thanks to the consumption of fatty tissue. What little urea is produced is recycled. The bear's kidneys release about one third of their normal summer capacity, and during hibernation this reduced amount is reabsorbed through the bladder wall where it is recycled and forms carbon dioxide, water, and ammonia.

The ammonia combines with glycerol (another fat by-product) to form amino acids, which in turn produce new proteins that are used to repair bones and other tissues where some protein loss has occurred. What is the result of all this recycling? During its five-to eight-month sleep, a bear doesn't have to urinate or defecate at all.

○ Black bears hibernate for varying lengths of time, depending on where they live. Some southern bears sleep only for a few days, while Alaska's black bears may disappear for three-quarters of the year. This remarkable form of hibernation has received much scientific attention. Scientists see possible links to kidney treatments and space exploration. Imagine the significance to the Mars space program if astronauts could hibernate for the journey there and back without losing bone mass.

Still, for all of this unique activity and physical change, the winter sleep of bears might not be considered nearly so remarkable if it wasn't for one other thing they do while in the den—the females give birth.

14 The Birth of Cubs

The conception, development, and birth of a bear's cubs are perhaps the most unusual in the mammal world. Sometime in the early summer the sow seeks out and finds a mate. Six or seven months later she gives birth during hibernation to two or three premature cubs. This pattern raises some fascinating questions. Why are the cubs premature if she has been carrying them for six months, and why give birth in winter instead of spring when there is food available?

If a cub were born in spring, it would face the insurmountable problem of gaining enough weight to go into hibernation the following winter. On the other hand, if a cub were born more fully developed in the den, feeding it would place too much demand on the sow's resources. For a spring birth, the ideal time to mate would be in the fall, but the demands of feeding at that time of year preclude sex. The bears simply do not have time to mate with winter quickly approaching.

So the bears mate in July, but the implantation of the fertilized egg (the blastocyst) is delayed until fall. The actual timing varies by location, climate, and the season's food resources. If, for any reason, a sow fails to put on enough weight, the embryo fails to attach to the uterine wall, and she breeds again next year.

If she does get enough fat stored, the premature cubs arrive two to three months later, sometime between late December and early February. The average birth date is mid-January. By giving birth at this time, the sow actually conserves energy—it takes less energy to suckle a cub than to nourish it through the placenta.

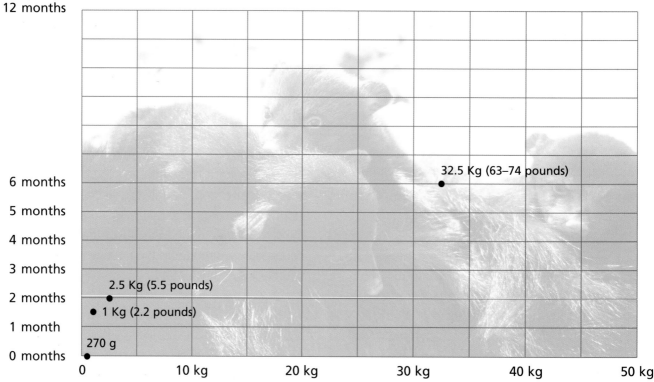

12 months	
6 months	32.5 Kg (63–74 pounds)
5 months	
4 months	
3 months	
2 months	2.5 Kg (5.5 pounds)
1 month	1 Kg (2.2 pounds)
0 months	270 g

0   10 kg   20 kg   30 kg   40 kg   50 kg

Bear cubs grow rapidly on a rich diet of bear milk.

Dr. Martyn Obbard and his assistant examine and tag these two-month-old cubs before returning them to the den.

The sow is usually partially awake for the birth, though she seems hardly aware of her labour. Once born, the cubs, usually twins or triplets, seek out their mother's nipples with no assistance from their mother. The hair around the nipples is very sparse, and they radiate more heat than other parts of the bear's body, drawing the cubs to this heat source. A sow has three pairs of functional nipples—two sets on her chest and one pair on her lower belly. By sleeping curled on her side, all six teats are drawn closer together, making it easier for the cubs to find them.

Newborns are blind and less than 16 centimetres (8 inches) long. They are covered with fine, gray hair and have poorly developed hindquarters, so they must drag themselves around using their front legs. They are also toothless.

At birth they weight only between 240 and 330 grams (16 and 20 ounces). This is roughly equal to 1/280th of their mother's weight. As a comparison, human newborns average about 1/25th of their mother's weight. Their growth rate, though, is astounding, as illustrated in the chart on facing page.

While they are in the den, the sow will eat the cub's feces. This may help reduce any telltale odours being released from the den that might attract predators. (There have been reports of wolves attacking bears in the den.) It also serves to keep the den clean.

Do Mother Bears Adopt?

Scientists have recently discovered that the sow's sense of smell functions poorly while she is in the den. They have used this knowledge to introduce orphaned cubs from other dens into an "adoption" site. A cub placed in or near the den opening will be rescued by its new "mother" and raised as one of her own.

Ontario predator biologist Dr. Martyn Obbard has placed orphaned cubs in another bear's den and has found it to be a moving experience. He crawled into the dens with the cub in hand and tried to gently place the cub on its new mother's chest. The sow usually looked on with some sleepy-eyed interest. Once, though, he dropped a cub, and the sow bared her teeth. "Oh oh", he thought, "She's going to kill it." Instead, she grabbed the orphan by the scruff of her neck and gently placed it on her chest.

Such events are probably rare in the wild. Bears do not usually den very close to each other, so it would be highly unlikely that a young cub would ever find its way to another bear's den without human help. A bear would naturally assume that any cub near its den was her own and would retrieve it.

After the family has left the den, it is a different story. A sow will kill any cubs that stroll by if her nose tells her that the cub is a stranger's. On the other hand, at the Vince Shute Wildlife Sanctuary in Minnesota, there have been several examples of females adopting cubs. It may be that a well-fed bear is more apt to do so, or it may be more common than biologists suspect.

Courtesy Dr. Martyn Obbard

15 Mothers and Cubs

When a sow emerges from the den in mid-spring, she will continue to fast for another two weeks. This is typical of both black and grizzly bears, male and female. It is a time when the bear's systems literally start up again. They continue to lose weight after hibernation and do not reach a balance between energy loss and food consumption until early to midsummer.

For the cubs, however, it is a different story. They continue to suckle throughout their first year and may even continue to do so occasionally into their second. The new cubs are the only ones to gain weight in the spring.

There are four possible food sources for the sow when she does start to eat. The most important of these are the green shoots of grasses, herbs, and leaves. New-growing plants are rich in food value. She will also look for any remaining nuts, raiding the caches of squirrels. Carrion and prey are the other two sources of food, but these are less reliable.

For the cubs, it is a period of learning and experimenting. They will chew on anything as their teeth erupt. They also observe what their mother does and will follow quite closely behind her. They sample and eat the various foods to which she guides them.

Mothers have been known to lead their young on treks of up to one hundred kilometres (60 miles) from their home ranges to show the cubs seasonal riches, such as a special berry patch or salmon run. These journeys often occur in the fall, when the bears are seeking the richest foods to fatten up for winter. The cubs remember these journeys and repeat them in later years.

This is a dangerous time for the young bears, and their mother is ever-watchful. The preferred escape route is up a tall tree where

A mother has sent her cubs scrambling up the trees to avoid danger.

Though the preferred behaviour is to retreat rather than confront, a mother will fight to the death to protect her cubs or yearlings, bravely challenging larger, more dominant bears.

they will be safer from larger black bears, wolves, and grizzlies. A specific sound from the mother bear is enough to send the cubs scrambling up a tree, although any perceived threat will cause them to climb. Once safe, they will wait patiently for their mother to call them down. She will also send them to a tree when she wants to go off and feed in an area that may be too dangerous for her babies.

A female bear is one of the most watchful and caring of mammalian mothers. Though the preferred behaviour is to retreat rather than confront, a mother will fight to the death to protect her cubs or yearlings, bravely challenging larger, more dominant bears. Her lower lip droops, and her upper lip extends. She bawls out a warning and holds her head low, ears back—she is ready to fight. The intruder must weigh the value of the food to be gained against the very real possibility that the mother will inflict serious wounds. If food is plentiful, the larger bear usually backs down.

As the cubs mature and fall approaches, they too begin to put on weight. When they enter the den with their mother, they must be fat enough to make it through the winter on their own. Their shared body heat helps, but they can expect little else from their mother. She cannot afford to nurse them this time.

Yearlings may den up with their mother again the next year if they live in poorer ranges or if she is not pregnant. These are the only times when large bears have been found denning together. Males usually leave after the first denning, although there are records of them staying near their mothers for up to four years.

Their journey away from home may take them over 100 kilometres (60 miles) from their birth den. Young male bears are by nature curious and aggressive—attributes that are critical if they are to establish a place for themselves in the forest. But such traits also expose them to danger. They may run afoul of wolves, male bears, traffic, hunters, and countless other natural hazards during their trek. Still, it is a journey they must make. The long trek ensures that when they reach sexual maturity in three or four years, there is little chance of courting either their mother or sisters.

Young cubs stay very close to their mother.

Above This very young cub is attempting to master the art of climbing.

Facing page These are all cubs-of-the-year, who will stay with their mother for at least one more denning season.

Left and below These cubs are at least yearlings, and maybe two years old.

A fifteen-year-old female may have produced as few as six litters in her lifetime. Very few of her offspring will survive to become adults.

Young females have it much easier. They will occupy part of their mother's home range. Although contact with her decreases rapidly in the second year, it is, for the most part, an amiable relationship. Their mother will even expand her territory to make more room for her daughters.

The size of the territory depends on the quality of the ecosystem, but on average runs between 15 and 25 square kilometres (6 to 10 square miles). While some females will allow some overlap in territories with other adult females, others will strongly defend their own—fights have been reported, even ending in death. Only if there is an abundance of food in a given location will they tolerate each other. In such cases, the two feeding families avoid close contact and keep a wary eye on each other. Anyone who has ever watched black bears at a dump has seen this behaviour in action.

All said, bears have the lowest reproductive rate of any of North America's land mammals, with the possible exception of the musk ox. A fifteen-year-old female may have produced as few as six litters in her life. Very few of her offspring will survive to become adults.

16 Mating Habits

A female black bear reaches sexual maturity in her third year. She will probably breed that year and once every two or three years after that. A major factor determining the age and frequency of breeding is the habitat—the richer the environment, the higher her reproductive success will be.

The first problem she must overcome is a rather basic one. She must find a male. This is not as easy as you might think. Black bears are, by nature, solitary, and are more accustomed to avoiding one another than seeking companionship. They have adapted to hiding in their habitat. Finding a mate in the forest can be a little like finding a needle in a haystack.

When in heat or estrus, the female becomes more restless and will travel the regular route through her home territory three times more rapidly than normal. This extra wandering increases the chance of meeting her mate. Another factor that works in her favour is the lengthy breeding season. Suitors are welcome from about the time she emerges from the den (usually May) until mid-July. The most active month is June.

The male bear is also actively seeking a mate at this time. He is capable of breeding from the age of three or four but rarely gets a chance

Eventually she attracts the attention of a male bear, but is he there for love or dinner? Big males have been known to kill and eat females so the courtship begins on a suspicious note.

Finding a mate in the forest can be a little like finding a needle in a haystack.

until he is able to hold his own against other adult males—usually around the eighth year.

An adult male has a range that will overlap the range of several females, and he will follow a scent until he comes across places where she has urinated. This clearly marks her path and allows other bears to know that this is her piece of countryside. During her limited breeding season, a hormone is released with her urine. At each scent post, the male will sniff for this telltale sign. Her vulva becomes swollen and

To attract a mate, the female dribbles hormone-scented urine as she walks her territory. After much posturing and bawling at each other, the female allows her suitor to come closer.

scent-marked as well. Eventually the two bears will meet.

Now the courting begins. At first she will retreat from the male, leading him on a merry chase. The distance will be allowed to shorten as it becomes clear that his intentions are

romantic and not dietary in nature. There follows a period of face-to-face encounters that, at first, appear like fights.

The female will only permit mating during the middle of her estrus period, those three to five days when she is most likely to conceive. During this time the two are inseparable. They feed together, bed together, and mate frequently.

The act of copulation takes about thirty minutes, but may last up to an hour. One theory for these lengthy encounters is that bears are

At first she will retreat from the male, leading him on a merry chase. The distance will be allowed to shorten as it becomes clear that his intentions are romantic and not dietary in nature.

He has finally convinced her that his intentions are honourable.

Sometimes rival males compete for the same female. Though it is possible for a serious fight to occur, one will usually retreat.

top predators and have little to fear from enemies. Wolves, also top predators, engage in prolonged intercourse as well. Prey species, such as deer, bison, and elk, all have very brief encounters. However, there are other top predators that mate briefly, such as African lions and other wild cats, and though weasels are in danger of being taken by foxes, owls, and hawks, they will mate for up to 90 minutes.

Another, more satisfactory theory is that long periods of copulation actually induce ovulation. Given the difficulties a sow experiences in finding a mate, it would be wasteful to release an egg without any chance of fertilization. By waiting for the stimulus brought about by contact with the male, the chance of wasting her reproductive energy is lessened.

Because finding a mate is so difficult, two or more males may find themselves competing for the same female. A smaller male will be chased off or may simply leave on his own. If the competing males are evenly matched, a bluff encounter may take place, and on rare occasions serious fighting occurs, sometimes resulting in severe wounds or death.

Once the mating period ends, the couple goes its separate ways. The male wanders off in search of another mate. The female may come into heat again in a month's time and may well find another mate as well. It is not unusual for her twins or triplets to have different fathers.

By the end of July sexual urges have subsided as the bears prepare for the winter.

17 Male Bears

Male bears are often reported to be "cub-killers." There is some truth to this, but not for the reason ordinarily thought. According to bear lore, males are so hungry that they will kill and eat their own offspring. While predation on cubs does occur (there are many well-documented cases of polar bears and grizzlies killing and eating other bears), the killing of cubs is usually linked to the male's reproductive needs.

A female bear will not come into heat as long as she is nursing because the production of milk inhibits ovulation. Should something happen to her cubs, though, her reproductive cycle will return as her milk dries up, and she will again seek a mate.

Although it is in the female's best interests to protect her cubs to ensure the passing on of her genes, the male's interests lie in breeding with as many females as possible. By killing a sow's cubs, the male encourages the female to breed. There is some likelihood of killing his own cubs as the male's range overlaps with that of several females, but no DNA research has been done to determine how often this occurs.

○ The killing of cubs by males may seem harsh by human standards, but there are several species that practice this behaviour, including lions, several species of monkeys, wild dogs, gorillas, hyenas, and even ground squirrels.

By killing a sow's cubs, the male encourages the female to breed.

Mothers with cubs avoid males as much as possible. When they do encounter them, their defence is so ferocious that the larger male usually backs down.

A sow charges a large male while her cub flees. Unless he is very hungry, he usually backs down from such a spirited defence.

In June, when they are one and one-half years old, most male cubs go their own way, wandering long distances. They are not only leaving their mothers, but their siblings as well, and they routinely fall prey to wolves, cougars, hunters, and accidents. If a bear survives this early period, it will likely lead a long and productive life.

Males do not stake out a territory like females, but instead range over a large area, on average 10 times the size of the females'. Thus, their home range will encompass that of several females as well as that of several other males. Bears use the same trails year after year. In some places, trails have been used for hundreds of years and are very well worn.

These young male bears are both on their own, but still young enough to enjoy a play fight. They may well be brothers.

Note the difference in size between a young adult male and a much older one. Both are standing by the same tree stump.

Though more tolerant of other males than females are of other females, males will usually deliberately avoid each other. Fresh droppings, tree scratches, and other scent posts alert them to the presence of another male. Normally, they just turn around and wander in another direction.

It is usually in the presence of a rich resource, like a berry patch or a single female, that they are likely to come into contact with another male. Where there is plentiful food, feigned indifference is the order of the day, and they will feed close together. However, with limited food resources or a female present, it is another matter. Although males reach sexual maturity at the same age as their sisters (at age three), it will be many years before they actually win the mating game—competition among males is intense, and a bear must have both the size and strength to dominate.

To a black bear, retreat is the better part of valour!

○ Cub killing is not a common occurrence. Although studies in Ontario and elsewhere have confirmed that it does happen, there is no evidence of it at the Vince Shute Wildlife Sanctuary in Minnesota, and it has been rarely documented at the McNeil River Sanctuary in Alaska. Large numbers of bears of all ages are observed at both locations.

18 Black Bears as Herbivores

○ Of the three North American species, the black bear consumes the greatest amount of vegetation, and the polar bear the least.

Though a carnivore by strict definition, 80 to 85 percent of the black bear's diet consists of plant material. The list of vegetation is long—generally, if it grows, the bear will eat it. There is, however, a pattern to its feeding. Some foods will be sought eagerly at one season and avoided the next. To understand why this is so, it is necessary to understand a little about the bear's digestive system.

Though a carnivore by strict definition, 80 to 85 percent of the black bear's diet consists of plant material.

True carnivores, such as wolves and pumas, have much shorter intestines than bears. It is in the intestines, not the stomach, where most of the food is digested. Meat, which is rich in carbohydrates and proteins, is digested quickly.

On the other hand, plant material, especially cellulose, resists breaking down. Thus, the bear's gut has become elongated, at least in comparison to the wolf's. The longer intestine allows more time for bacteria to break down the plant material. This adaptation allows bears to gain nourishment from plants, and is the secret to their success as omnivores.

Compared to true herbivores though, their digestion is not really very efficient. Large ungulates, such as bison, deer, cattle, horses, and zebras, have more highly developed digestive systems and absorb between 45 and 60 percent of the food they eat. Bears, on the other hand, are lucky to get 25 percent of the energy available. Where the ungulates can derive nourishment out of poor quality food, even in winter, bears cannot and look for only those plants highest in carbohydrates and proteins.

In spring, they will feed on the first tender grass shoots, spring flowers, leaf buds, skunk cabbage, catkins, and young leaves. This period of early growth is often referred to by ecologists as the green-up. These plants have not yet had time for the cellulose to become firm. This allows the bears to get maximum energy with comparatively little time spent with food in their digestive tract. Once the plants have matured, the food value is minimal.

In spring, black bears will begin feeding on the warmer, exposed slopes, meadows, and glades where plants first appear. They then follow the spring green-up growth into more shaded valleys and cooler forests where the process is slower. This food is important to the bears to restart their bodies after the long period of hibernation. They do not gain weight during this period, but rather eat enough to maintain their bodies and meet their energy requirements as they go about their business.

Black bears will also feed on the bark of trees and the soft, growing, cambium layer underneath. Tree sap can be important at this time of year too. In fact, tree damage caused by bears is significant in some parts of their range, especially in the west.

By summer they turn their attention to the soft-mast: the berries. Virtually everywhere in a black bear's range there are some kind of berries growing—blueberries, huckleberries, June berries, raspberries, bearberries, cherries, strawberries, soapberries, hawberries, cranberries, and Saskatchewan berries. All are high-energy sources of food and are essential for the bear's survival, for the berries are what causes the bears to begin gaining weight for their winter sleep.

The fall hard-mast of nuts is also important for gaining weight. In the northeast, black bears can look forward to dining on acorns, beechnuts, and hickory nuts. In the west, coniferous nuts, particularly the whitebark pine nuts, are a favourite. They will also raid the middens (food storage areas) of ground squirrels and devour their store of nuts. One bear

Bears replenish their energy after hibernation with new spring grasses.

was observed polishing off 3,000 hazelnuts in one day—many of them from the caches of squirrels. Oak stands in Riding Mountain

How's Your Digestion?

Ungulates approach and even exceed bears in size. They survive on a diet of plant material alone. They do not hibernate, and they outnumber the bear populations by hundreds to one. Why are they so much more successful than bears? It has to do with their digestive tracts.

There are two basic ungulate body plans. The even-toed order, Artiodactyls, consists of bison, deer, antelope, cattle, sheep, and goats. They have two toes on each hoof and are known for their "four stomachs." It is the first of those four stomachs, the rumen, that is really the secret to their success. This organ gives them the other family name by which they are known: ruminant.

The rumen is more of a storage container than a stomach. When plant material is swallowed, it sits in the rumen for some time. During this period, bacteria begin the process of breaking it down into accessible carbohydrates and proteins.

After the plant material has sat for a while in the rumen, the animal regurgitates a lump of it into its mouth and re-chews it. Cud chewing, as this is known, hastens the breakdown of fibres, and when the food is swallowed again it is ready to pass through the other three stomachs where digestion is completed. About 60 percent of the plant material is absorbed.

The odd-toed ungulates, the order Perissodactyls, consist of horses, zebras, tapirs, and rhinoceroses. They have only one stomach and most of their digestion takes place in the intestines and cecum. They absorb about 45 percent of the food they eat but process it almost twice as fast as the ruminants do. They do not chew cud.

Above Bears, as well as bison and other herbivores, feed in the meadows and glades where the spring green-up is rich with new plant life.

Bears feed on a large variety of berries, including blueberries, raspberries, and hawberries (insert). Blueberries are an important summer crop for bears. If the crop fails, they may come into town seeking alternate foods.

Left A mother demonstrates to her cubs the fine art of dining on leaves and twigs.

Bears often raid the caches of squirrels.

National Park in Manitoba provide enough food during a good growing season for the bears to put on a kilogram a day!

In the south, where many of the oak stands and other nut-bearing trees have been removed, black bears have turned to a diet of needle palm, palmetto, and tupelo berries.

Bears feed during the day, but in those regions where they are hunted, they have become nocturnal feeders.

The role of omnivore has allowed the black bear to become the most successful large carnivore in North America. Unlike the wolf, it is not viewed as a threat to game species and therefore has benefitted from a more tolerant attitude from its human neighbours. Wolves, especially in the United States, were hunted almost to extinction because farmers and ranchers feared they would prey on domestic animals. Bears suffered from this type of persecution as well but not nearly as much as the wolf.

Left After the lower branches are stripped of berries, the bear will reach for less accessible ones.

19 Black Bears as Carnivores

Only 15 percent of a black bear's diet is made up of animal protein. Though this is a small proportion, it is significant, since the amount of protein contained in animal matter is far greater than that in a similar amount of vegetative matter.

Bears, in general, are not suited for the type of hunting that wolves and mountain lions do. Because they are flat-footed, bears are not fast runners and are ill-suited for long chases. Nor are they socially cooperative the way wolves are. And, by virtue of their size, they are not especially well suited for stalks or ambushes such as those practiced by the large cats.

The truth is that much of the animal matter that black bears consume is in the form of insects. To a bear, there is nothing like the crunchy grubs of ants for a satisfying midday snack. Another favourite food is the tent caterpillar. These insects erupt every few years in huge numbers and bears feast on them. In one study, bears ate 25,000 caterpillars per day.

The truth is that much of the animal matter that black bears consume is in the form of insects.

Bees and their honey have long held a popular place in the public image of a bear's diet. Honeybees are not native to North America and represent a new source of food. They were imported from Europe to New England in 1638 to produce honey as a sweetener. It has become a double delicacy for the bears—a source of honey and insect grubs—and bears a major irritant to bee farmers.

A native American bee, the bumblebee, is also a source of grubs. Bees offer a spirited defence of their nests, but their stings are not especially effective deterrents against marauding bears. Only the eyes, nose, and lips of the bear are exposed to provide a reasonable target for the bees, and the bears seem able to ignore the pain inflicted long enough to get what they want.

Any insect, however, is a target. During their rambles through the forest, bears are constantly turning over rocks and ripping open rotten logs to slurp up whatever treats crawl out.

Carrion is equally appealing, even more so if it has developing fly larvae in it. A high proportion of meat in a bear's diet is from animals the bear did not kill.

Caterpillars are a real pest for landowners, but a real treat for bears.

The stings of the honey bee are of minor concern to a bear bent on honey or grubs.

Bears are not picky eaters—carpenter ants provide a rich source of protein.

Still, black bears are predators. If an opportunity presents itself, they will hunt and kill their own prey. A distracted large mammal that wanders too close to a bear is fair game. Injured animals are easily taken. In both cases, the black bear is an opportunist, taking advantage of the circumstances. Small mammals, especially beavers that venture too far from water to cut a tree, are at risk. A bear will not pass up a nest of young voles or mice, bird eggs, or young birds. Even an unwary fox, cougar, or a wolf cub may become dinner.

Moose, elk, and caribou calves, and whitetail and mule deer fawns are all popular menu

Nests of eggs or young birds are easy targets for a bear in search of food. Bears will also eat young meadow voles, mice or other small creatures that they stumble across.

Beavers can fall prey to black bears if they go too deep into the forest searching for the ideal tree for their dam.

Elk calves in the west are easily taken. The mothers will try to defend their young, but the defence is often too little too late.

items for bears. They are not chance victims. Bears will patrol the calving areas—meadows and glades where such prey is commonly found. For the first few days of their lives, young white-tailed deer, mule deer, and elk are left hidden in forest glades or long grass. Unable to outrun a predator, their defence is to lie still and hope the predator does not see them. When they are born, their mothers lick them clean and eat the afterbirth to reduce any telltale scents that may give away their hiding sites. Deer fawns and elk calves are virtually scentless, but they do produce enough of an

odour for the bear's sensitive nostrils to detect. Moose and caribou do not use this strategy. Their calves follow their mothers within a few hours of birth.

The larger mothers may well succeed in saving their young. They will chase after and slash at the bear with their sharp front hooves. Moose put up the best defence, and if there is only one calf, they usually succeed in driving off the bruin, but if there are twins, one is likely to fall prey. According to Pat Russo, a warden at Riding Mountain National Park, elk do not put up a very spirited defence; deer are even less able to fend off a bear.

The number of calves lost can be quite high. In an Idaho study, 47 of the 53 radio-collared

Moose have the best luck defending their young against black bears, but a mother is seldom able to successfully defend twins.

Deers are least able to fend off a bear.

elk calves that died were taken by black bears. When 65 percent of the black bear population was removed to other locations, calf survival was much higher. Studies of black bear predation on moose calves in Alaska, Saskatchewan, and Quebec revealed that about one third of radio-collared calves were taken by bears—a lower proportion due to the moose's larger size.

Bears have always enjoyed feasting on salmon in West Coast streams. In times of good runs, the bear is a sloppy feeder, often leaving most of the carcasses for other scavengers. However, the recent decline in salmon numbers because of overfishing has greatly reduced this rich source of protein.

Domestic animals have certainly been taken. Range sheep, cattle, swine, and even horses have occasionally been killed by black bears. In fairness to the bears, though, in the majority of cases where bears have fed on domestic animals, the animals likely died a natural death or were taken down by other predators. The black bear may well have been feeding on carrion when discovered by the irate rancher.

Is bear predation a serious problem? That answer depends on your point of view. Hunters and trappers might well argue that the loss of game animals and furbearers to bears constitutes serious competition. Loggers argue virtually the same thing in areas where bears kill trees. Naturalists and biologists would argue that the bear is merely fulfilling its role in the ecosystem. To date, the bear has been the win-

Fish are a rich source of protein, but West Coast salmon numbers have gone down, and only now do they seem to be increasing slowly.

ner in these debates. In fact, its value as a hunting species has also helped it. Some Canadian provinces once treated the bear as vermin and allowed a ten-month hunting season with few controls on the age, sex, or size taken. When the economic value of the species as a trophy for United States' hunters became apparent, hunting seasons and management plans were put into place. As a result, bear numbers increased.

Do Bears Attack Full-grown Moose?

Do black bears prey on adult moose? Only one case has been documented. A radio-collared male bear in Ontario's Chapleau study area apparently came upon a cow moose in her day bed. The boar leapt on her back and, despite the cow's desperate attempt to dislodge it by crashing into trees, the bear was able to bring the cow down. Biologists were able to reconstruct the events from tracks and other signs. Subsequent work on the bone marrow of the moose indicated that she was in good health. Such attacks are believed to be rare.

20 Scatology

The study of animal droppings—scatology—has long been our window into an animal's lifestyle. Just as doctors will request a sample of human waste to analyze for disease, so too can a scatologist glean information about the health of an animal. They can also determine what the animal ate, something of its size, and, of course, what species it is.

Bear droppings, when firm, are tubular and look much like human droppings. This is no surprise, as both species are omnivores and have similar-sized digestive tracts. Like bears, humans must eat foods that are high in nutritional value. Neither species can process foods of low value. This explains why bears are drawn to our garbage and food supplies—our processed food is ideal for them.

Most bear droppings found in the woods consist of plant material. This can give a false impression of a bear's diet because plant material is poorly digested compared to a dinner of meat. Meat stools are runny and quickly absorbed into the soil. Plant stools last longer due to the tough cellulose material that survives the passage through the bear's gut.

Bear scat will vary according to the type of

Humans and bears have similar digestive systems—no wonder they are attracted to our processed foods.

◯ A Word of Caution

Great care should be used in examining any species' droppings. All contain bacteria that could be harmful to humans. Scatologists and biologists wear surgical masks and collect samples in sealed plastic bags for examination later. Prior to working with the scat, it is sterilized to destroy the bacteria. If you must examine a dropping in the wild, use a stick to break it up or turn it over.

food eaten. Strawberries may produce a very runny pile, while spring grass produces a more solid, greenish stool. Often it is possible to recognize the berries or the shell of seeds the dropping contains. Hair indicates that the bear was feeding on a kill or carrion. Sometimes even the odour of the scat will give its makeup away—there might be a scent of blueberry or raspberry to it.

These piles on the forest floor serve to promote the spread of plants through the environment. The seeds of many berries and fruits are coated with protective shells and resins that resist the bear's gastric attempts to break them down. They pass intact, and small mammals, birds, and insects will eat them, thus spreading the seeds even wider. Seeds that are left benefit from a rich, warm, moist pile of manure in which to germinate—the perfect fertil-

Top to bottom: **This scat is from a black bear that had a hankering for apples. It's not pretty, but the only other ways of determining a bear's diet is to follow it for hours, or shoot it to examine the contents of its stomach!**

These are likely wild raspberry seeds. Such a pile could contain hundreds, if not thousands, but one is disinclined to count them.

This runny scat is characteristic of a bear that has been eating meat.

The bear that produced these droppings was feeding on green leaves that contained a fair amount of moisture.

izer. Given that bears spend most of their active periods eating, the number of seeds they spread plays an important role in the ecology of an area.

These "bear gardens," as the researchers call them, are often the site of intense competition among germinating plants. Only the strong will survive. However, rain will break down the stool, spreading out the seeds and providing them with a better opportunity to germinate. Although birds have been thought to be the prime distributors of plant seeds, it appears that bears may be even more effective at performing this task, at least within their "seed shadow."

A seed shadow is the area over which a bear deposits its seed-bearing scat. The average length of time for a seed to stay in a bear's digestive tract is 24 hours. Within that time the bear may roam many kilometres, helping to ensure the genetic diversity of plant species. Part of their wanderings will take bears across barren landscapes, such as mountain talus (rocks at the base of a cliff), dried streambeds, avalanche sights, or burned out areas. Like birds, the bruins are bringing colonizing plants to these lifeless areas.

Some of the most interesting bear scats are produced soon after emerging from the den. They are usually hard and dry, giving rise to the notion of a fecal plug, which, as one theory goes, develops in the bowel at the time of hibernation, perhaps as a method of preventing contamination of either the den or the bowel tract itself. A more likely explanation is that this hard scat, which consists of hair, grass, leaves, and twigs, is simply the dried, undigested remains of the bear's last meal prior to entering the den.

Bears, of course, get information from the waste deposits of their own kind. Urine and droppings serve to mark their wanderings, alerting other bears to their presence.

Although birds have been thought to be the prime distributors of plant seeds, it appears that bears may be even more effective at performing this task, at least within their "seed shadow."

21 Sign Language

Black bears leave a wide variety of signs during their wanderings. Naturalists, bear biologists, and hunters have a stake in learning to read these clues to bear behaviour.

Here are some signs to watch for:

TRACKS

Black bear tracks are always exciting to find because they are rare—it takes luck and special circumstances. Look for them along wet trails, in mud, along beaches, and especially along the sides of dirt roads. You may see fresh tracks along rocks if their feet were wet.

Bears are "plantigrade" walkers, like us. That is, they walk with the entire sole of their feet on the ground, not on their toes as do dogs and cats. There is something distinctly "human" about a bear's track, especially the imprint left by the rear feet.

In areas where both black bears and grizzlies co-exist, it is helpful to know which bear you are following. The chart below suggests ways of identifying the maker of the track, but these are guidelines only. When trying to determine which species made the track, consider all the information you can glean from the track, and then consider other evidence. Is the habitat more suited for black or grizzly? Which species is more common in the area?

Comparing Tracks	Adult Black Bear	Yearling Grizzly/ Brown Bear	Adult Grizzly Brown Bear
Position of small toe	behind the leading edge of the palm pad	in front of the leading edge of the palm pad	in front of the leading edge of the palm pad
Claw length	usually shorter than the toe length	often longer than the toe length	often longer than the toe length
Fore feet length:	12.7–16 cm (5–6.25 in.)	14.6–16.5 cm (5.75-6.5 in.)	17.8–34.3 cm (7–13.5 in.)
width:	9.5–14 cm (3.75–5.5 in.)	12–14.6 cm (4.75–5.7 in.)	12.7–22.2 cm (5–8.75 in.)
Hind feet length:	15.2–19.5 cm (6-7.75 in.)	21–25 cm (8.25–9.75 in.)	21–35.6 cm (8.25–14 in.)
width:	9–14 cm (3.5–5.5 in.)	12.7–14.6 cm (5–5.75 in.)	11.7–21.6 cm (4.5–21.6 in.)
Stride length from front foot to other front foot when walking	43.2–63.5 cm (17–25 in.)	Highly variable depending on region, age. Use position of small toe and claw length to determine species. 48.3–73.7 cm (19–29 in.)	48.3–73.7 cm (19–29 in.)

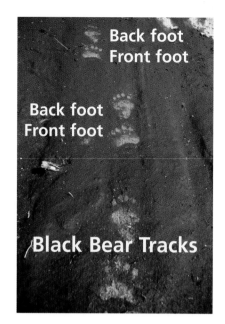

Back foot
Front foot

Back foot
Front foot

Black Bear Tracks

The hind foot appears directly in front of the front foot. The hind paw makes a full print, while the front paw does not.

A black bear print embedded in mud.

Follow that bear, if you dare!

Below An overturned rock marks the spot where a bear fed on bugs and worms.

Bears wiggle when they walk. This is because they are somewhat pigeon-toed, with their feet pointing inwards. The walking pattern is both right legs forward, then both left legs forward. The rear foot lands in front of or close to where the front foot was placed. As a result, the front footprint is normally behind the rear footprint. The normal stride of a walking black bear ranges from 43.2 to 63.5 centimetres (17 to 25 inches). A running bear's is nearly twice as long.

DIGGING
Look for places where a bear has been digging up grubs and insects. They will turn over rocks, scrape away the ground cover, and rip apart logs as they dig out beetle larvae.

CLIMBING TREES
Bears are great climbers, but finding their marks on most trees is very difficult. One species, the American beech, preserves the bears' adventures very clearly. The tree has a cork-like bark that scars easily as the bear climbs. When the tree heals, dark wounds

remain where the bears' claws penetrated.

Unfortunately, it is difficult to tell how fresh these marks are, but Mark Elbroch, in his excellent book on tracking, *Mammal Tracks and Sign*, provides some guidance. Tracks up to three years old will generally leave an orange to brown scar, and the edges will have no height. Marks from three to seven years old will likely be gray to black in colour with some cracking in the scar. The older the track marks, the more heightening around the edges, and they will have widened.

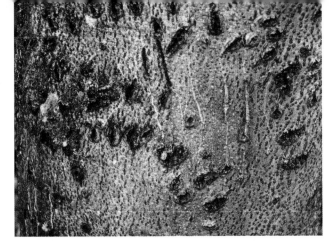

A tree retains a record of the bears that have climbed it to feast on its mast of beechnuts.

The attraction is, of course, the beechnuts. Bears love these sweet nuts, but the mast or nut crop is not an annual occurence. Several years may pass before a stand of trees produces a sizeable mass.

Bears have very good hearing and can come down a tree very quickly, so your chances are slim of catching one up tree. They feel trapped up there and prefer to slip off unseen.

TREE NESTS

Look for these in beech trees and other trees where nuts have ripened. But the word "nest" is misleading—they are not true nests. Bears do not sleep in them. In fall, they build a platform from branches that they strip the nuts from. Nests can

A bear "nest" adorns the top of a beech tree. It does not serve as a nest for sleeping, but is used as a platform for feeding.

last a season or two before the weight of snow or strong winds bring them down.

SCRATCHING TREES

Bears will claw a tree, leaving deep marks in the bark. One theory for this behaviour is that they are marking their territory and letting other bears know how tall they are.

DENS

Bears' dens are usually well hidden and look like any other mound of snow in the forest. Look for the telltale breathing hole, where frost crystals will have formed from the bear's warm, moist breath. Don't assume that the den is directly beneath the breathing hole, as the warm air may have travelled some distance before finding a weakness in the snow cover.

Even for trained bear biologists, locating a bear's den is very difficult. Radio telemetry has proved very useful in such a search.

A bear has stripped away the bark from this tree.

Any mound of snow could be covering a bear's den. Look for the telltale breathing hole.

Skeletal remains may be a sign that bears were about, but it is difficult to tell which predator was at work, so it helps to know who the neighbours are.

22 The Black Bear's Neighbours

Black bears interact with a variety of other species. Their role as predators is discussed in Chapter 19, but they also fall prey to other animals.

Wolves will kill unprotected bear cubs, and experts believe cougars will as well. In 1998, park wardens in Yellowstone National Park (Wyoming) reported the probable killing of an adult male black bear by a grizzly. This likely occurs throughout the northwest.

There are occasional reports of grizzlies killing black bears.

Pat Russo, a warden at Riding Mountain National Park in Manitoba, cited two cases where wolves preyed upon black bears. Both, however, were injured from a previous accident or fight, and were attacked by the wolves while in their dens. When injured, bears give off a sweet, sickly smell that even humans, let alone wolves, can detect.

The list of potential enemies can be surprising. In the southern parts of their range, alligators take the occasional bear. Bald eagles and golden eagles certainly have the strength to pick up a cub that strays too far from its mother.

Bald eagles present a threat to small cubs.

Domestic dogs can also be a threat—packs of them running free are more than capable of killing small bears.

Poisonous snakes will bite a bear that wanders too close, and bears that get too close to porcupines may wind up with a snout full of quills that can quickly become infected.

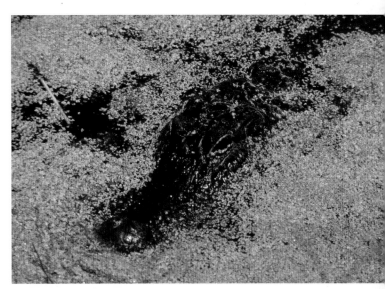

Alligators share much of their range with black bears and have been known to attack them.

Massassauga rattlesnakes are found in much of the eastern range of black bears and are always ready to defend themselves against larger intruders if they can't escape.

Some very small life forms rely on bears for their existence. Internal parasites and blood-sucking insects both live off the bear's body. Chiggers, a type of mite, like to attach themselves to, and dine on, the bear's skin. The itching sensation they create likely explains why bears love a good scratch. Ticks also find the bear a generous host and feed on the bear's blood in early summer.

Humans are not the only ones driven mad by mosquitoes. Black bears will take to the trees where there is wind to blow the mosquitoes away. Brown bears rarely stop to feed, but eat on the run when the bugs are bad. Polar bears resort to snowy patches or gravel beds where either cold or wind will rid them of the little monsters. If all else fails, a dip in the water works for all three.

The black bear plays a highly beneficial role within the ecosystem. If it makes a kill, foxes, weasels, and birds scavenge the remains. A bear's droppings, aside from dispersing seeds for new growth to distant areas, provides some rodents with a good meal. A bear feeding on acorns in the treetops will dislodge the nuts, providing a meal for deer and other animals below that are unable to climb.

Bears also open pathways through the for-est by continually using the same trails. These well-worn paths are used by a variety of species, including humans. Bears likely made many of the trails used by Aboriginal peoples and settlers from Europe.

On the other hand, other species provide many benefits for bears. Beavers are constantly altering the landscape—their dams cause floods in the forest when new, and meadows when the dams break down and the water drains away. It is these meadows, especially in the east, that provide bears with their first taste of spring grasses.

Beavers help create habitat for black bears and sometimes provide a good meal as well.

The red fox shares much of the black bear's habitat and may benefit from scavenging the remains of a bear's kill.

23 The Growing Numbers of Bears

In the wild, black bears can live up to 25 years, but few do. In addition to hunting, poaching, and numerous predators, bears also fall victim to starvation, drought, and accidents. It's a wonder that their population is, in fact, growing.

The increase in the continent's number of black bears has been phenomenal. Appendices I and II list black bear numbers in U.S. states and Canadian provinces and territories for five different years, from 1966 to 2003. Mexico also has a small black bear population, but there are no estimates available. In 1966 there were an estimated 148,533 black bears living in the United States. No figures were available for Canada that year, but it is believed that there were at least as many, and possibly double the number. Thus, there were likely between 300,000 and 450,000 black bears in North America.

Record keeping has improved since then, and estimates for both countries are available. Growth during the 1980s in the U.S. was astounding, more than doubling—almost catching up to the growing numbers in Canada.

The increase in the continent's number of black bears has been phenomenal.

During the 1990s there was a continuing, but less dramatic, increase. The U.S. figures rose by 16 percent, and Canada's by 20 percent. By 2003, the total North American population was estimated at 876,000, but this figure falls between high and low numbers cited. There could be as many as one million black bears alive in North America today!

The growth in the United States numbers requires some clarification. A large portion of this increase has taken place in Alaska, where, like Canada, much of it is still wild. However, the U.S. growth without Alaska is still substantial. The numbers rose from 128,000 in 1966 to 289,552 in 2003—more than double the population south of the 49th parallel in less than forty years!

Estimates of Black Bear Populations (based on the data in Appendices I and II)

Date Data Collected	United States	Canada	Total
1966	151,000	150,000 to 300,000*	300,000 to 450,000
1977	185,000	334,000	513,000
early 1993	362,000	390,0000	752,000
2003	434,000	437,000	871,000

* estimate only (no data collected)

Strangely, in the province of Alberta, there appears to have been a large decrease in black bear numbers, from 100,000 in 1977 to 36,000 today. How can we explain this massive drop, when the general trend has been an increase? Researchers believe that the original number estimated was far too high, based on faulty data. British Columbia's figure for 1977 was also 100,000, and it has much more habitat area. Alberta's black bears are not found on the prairie, which makes up almost one quarter of the province's area. In contrast, almost one hundred percent of B.C. is suitable habitat for black bears, and some of it, along the coast, is among the best in North America.

But what accounts for the apparently dramatic increase in the number of black bears in North America? It is likely that the figures for today's population are more accurate than earlier figures for a number of reasons: better management techniques, better census methods, and more researchers. Increased public interest has spurred on research, as well as the recognition back in the 1960s of the species as a game animal. Hunters were willing to spend big bucks to hunt the black bear, and states and provinces needed to know how many bears they had to better manage the population. Also, many universities now have graduate and undergraduate students working on black bear research. The result is that we know a lot more about black bears and their activities—and we have a more accurate estimate of their numbers.

○ Bears were once thought of as varmints and eliminated without much public concern. Characters like Smokey the Bear, Yogi, and Gentle Ben helped capture the public's attention, with the result that bear research sponsored by state, provincial, and national governments has been ongoing.

Not only are their numbers up, but their range is expanding as well. There are now black bears in some states where they have been absent for decades. Massachusetts reported no bears in 1966 or 1977. Now they report some 2,000! Nevada had none in the first year of the survey, 24 in 1977, and 350 in 2002. North Dakota has gone from zero to 250.

○ Bears are being reported with increasing frequency, even in the vicinity of Toronto, a city of over three million people. By 1999 researchers were reporting between 75,000 and 100,000 bears in Ontario.

There could be as many as one million black bears alive in North America today!

But how do researchers study population growth? Today, collared animals transmit to satellites, which are monitored by researchers often hundreds of kilometres away. Not only has the technique improved from the days of going into the field to count animals, but it has also become more affordable.

If researchers know how many radio-collared animals there are in a study area, they can begin to estimate the population. Elk populations are estimated using the same approach. For example, if researchers see 10 elk for every one radio-collared elk they see, and they know there are 10 collared ones, then they can estimate there are 100 elk in that area.

This use of radio telemetry has been invaluable in unlocking the secrets of the black bear's unseen forest world. Den sites are located, ranges mapped, and individuals followed. This, coupled with other, more traditional methods, has helped to eliminate the "educated guesses."

Bacon Bait for a Tetracycline Study

Minnesota's Department of Natural Resources (MDNR) approached the bear census problem in a unique way: bacon baits! Actually, the bacon bait was just a ploy to get the bears to eat tetracycline. When ingested, tetracycline marks the animal's bones and teeth, and those markings are used to estimate population size. How well did it work? An inquiry brought the following answer: "In 1997, bears ate 1,277 of the 3,000 + tet-laced baits put out. We [MDNR] later collected bone samples from hunters and found that 7 percent had double tet-marks (meaning bears that consumed 2 baits), so we converted the 1,277 baits consumed to 1,193 different bears that consumed tetracycline. That is, the population had 1,193 tet-marked bears. We collected 4,701 bone samples from hunters, of which 244, or 5.2 percent, had tet-marks. Thus, the 1,193 marked bears represented 5.2% of the population, and so the population is about 1,193 / .052 = 23,000 bears. It turns out that this number was within 500 bears of the number we estimated through population modeling. It represents significant growth (about 7 percent per year) since our last tet-based population estimate of 15,600 in 1991. We now believe the population is about 29,000."

These bears are wild and free-roaming. They have been brought together by an abundant food source. Such a gathering is called a "sleuth" of bears.

24 Adapting to a Changing Habitat

Why are black bear numbers increasing in the United States? In the 1800s and early 1900s, bear numbers dropped as they were either killed or forcibly ejected from much of their former range as land was cleared to make room for farms and homesteads. However, following that period of agricultural growth came a change in the cultural makeup of the U.S. that saw more people leaving rural communities to work in cities.

Canada experienced the same trend, but it was confined to the more temperate southern parts of the country where agriculture could be supported. In the 1800s in Ontario, 3 percent of the population lived in cities and towns, while 97 percent lived off the land. By the 1980s, those numbers were reversed and 97 percent of the population lived in urban centres.

As people left the land to live in large communities, the forests began to regenerate. These young forests are providing increasingly better habitats for bears where once they had been only marginal. White-tailed deer and wild turkeys were also quick to move in.

Attitudes toward bears were changing as well. In the early parts of the 19th century, bearskin was a popular fur item, but the trade fell by 1840 when the European market for

As more and more farms revert back to bush, bears reclaim the land.

beaver and other North American fur declined. Farmers also posed a threat, viewing bears as a danger to both livestock and crops, and bounties were posted. New York State dropped its bounty in 1904, but other states persisted until as late as 1965.

Many places continued to view bears as varmints and had few controls on hunting seasons, even though bounties were no longer being paid. In Ontario, hunting was widespread until the early 1980s. Many Americans came north, keen to hunt black bear as a game animal, and this market helped convince the provincial legislature that better management techniques were required. When they enacted laws giving the black bear game status, they were following a trend most other states and provinces had already adopted.

Game status confers certain protections. Seasons can be closed if necessary to allow low numbers of animals to increase to viable populations again. The age, sex, and number of animals killed can be regulated as well.

The establishment of protected parkland also helped preserve remnant populations from which the numbers could regenerate. The establishment of Great Smoky Mountains National Park in 1940 in the mountains of Georgia, North Carolina, and Tennessee is one such place. Other protected areas included Adirondack State Park in New York State and Florida's Everglades National Park.

New logging practices have also indirectly encouraged a growth in black bear numbers. Bears avoided clear-cuts of over 25 acres—such areas were common in the old days of logging. As an enlightened lumber industry created smaller, wildlife-friendly cutting methods, the bears benefited from increased berry and green growth.

Bears, though they live near people, tend to avoid them, but what do you do when one comes knocking at your door?

As an enlightened lumber industry created smaller, wildlife-friendly cutting methods, the bears benefited from increased berry and green growth.

A major threat to the bear is the automobile. In some areas, underpasses are being constructed to provide safe crossings for bears and other wildlife.

In addition, the black bear's ability to get along with people, or at least to avoid confrontations, has served them well. Studies in Pennsylvania and Minnesota have shown that black bears are able to live virtually unnoticed among fairly large human populations. Bear sightings in Canadian cities such as Vancouver, Calgary, and North Bay are common, and while many such sightings are caused by the failure of berry crops, there is little doubt that bears live close to city boundaries, usually out of sight.

Finally, several states have moved to reintroduce black bears into their jurisdictions without much negative attention, or to fully protect the few bears that are still present. Plans to reintroduce the wolf to western states have not been as welcome.

There are many areas of concern that could reverse these trends. Urban sprawl on restored farmland will shrink the bear's habitat, as will increased road traffic. Illegal poaching also poses a problem. So far, however, bear numbers are on the increase, and this is a trend that pleases naturalists, hunters, and biologists alike.

25 Black Bears as a Game Species

Black bears have been hunted in North America for thousands of years. While never as popular as deer, elk, or bison, they nonetheless were an important source of fat, tallow, meat, and hides for people who lived off the forested land. Today, people hunt for a variety of reasons. Bear meat is considered to be of good quality, if a little on the greasy side. Trophy hunting for the hide and skull is another reason. Some hunters do it for the thrill of bringing down a potentially dangerous animal. Still others just enjoy the experience of stalking and hunting, the kill itself being anticlimactic.

A recent publication indicated that there are now about 32,000 black bears killed annually by licenced hunters in North America. Every Canadian province (except Prince Edward Island, where there are no black bears) and territory and 26 U.S. states have hunting seasons.

Virtually all of these jurisdictions have bear management programs in place, and hunter success rate is carefully monitored. With few exceptions, the limit is one bear per person per year, and many jurisdictions impose other limits, such as the method of hunting.

Today, black bears are hunted by one of several traditional methods. Not all of these methods are necessarily allowed in each location.

Baiting bears is popular in many locations. The hunter usually stations himself in cover or in a tree stand nearby. A platform is located in a sturdy tree close to where the bait is placed. Most animals, including bears, seldom look up for danger, so the raised stand is an ideal hiding spot. The bait generally consists of foods with enticing odours—suet, spoiled meat, vegetables, and fruit are all used to attract a bear.

Amateur photographers should note that bear baiting can be dangerous—the bear may view the photographer as competition for its food. However, in the past few years, several locations in both Canada and the United States have opened bear-viewing sites that bait the area to bring the bears in. In one spot, guests are escorted onto bleachers to view the bears in safety.

Running bears with dogs is also allowed in some places. Trained hounds are released on the trail of the animal, and hunters follow along until the bear either climbs a tree or stands its ground. Dogs can be seriously injured if they corner the bear before it is shot.

Although seldom used, calling bears is increasing in popularity. There is a bear call being marketed that imitates the sound a cub makes when it is afraid. It is reported to bring in both females and males. Bears will also come to predator calls and even turkey calls.

○ Calling, in some national parks, is banned because a photographer was seriously injured by a grizzly bear he had called in. Remember that any bear that comes to such a call is responding to gain food or to protect a cub. It may well be agitated and therefore dangerous.

Bears are sometimes stalked, or shot from canoes. Guides have been known to fly over the forest and note tree damage done by bears feeding on acorn or other nut mast, and then direct clients to that area.

Seasons for bear hunts vary. A bear killed in the spring, soon after emerging from its winter sleep, may lack weight but its winter coat still

has a good shine to it. By the time bears molt in late May or June, though, the hunt is pretty much over.

In Ontario, the government, as a result of pressure from the public, cancelled the spring bear hunt, concerned that hunters shooting mothers by mistake were orphaning bear cubs. This action was taken despite advice from research biologists, who believe that ending the spring bear hunt would have little impact on cub survival.

The cancellation of the spring hunt has apparently resulted in an increase in black bear numbers. Again, there is no direct evidence, but a series of dry summers and the resulting failure of wild berry crops have likely contributed to more sightings. In 2003 the Nuisance Bear Review Committee set up by the Ontario Ministry of Natural Resources found no link to the ending of the spring bear hunt and the increased number of nuisance bear reports. Their conclusion was that lack of wild food caused the bears to seek alternative sources.

It is often difficult to tell a male from a female, but a nursing sow's nipples are quite prominent.

Most areas protect females with cubs, but it is very difficult for a hunter to accurately determine the sex of a black bear. However, if cubs are present, it is most likely the mother nearby, as cubs never venture too near a male. Mature adult male black bears are larger and heavier than females, and they have a more massive head. Their snouts are broader and, because of the size of their heads, their ears appear smaller than a female's. However, young males look very much like females. A nursing mother's nipples are often easy to spot, and the male's testicles and penis are visible under the right conditions, for example, if he stands and faces the observer. The problem is that these telltale signs are often not evident during a hunt until it is too late.

Biologists are trying to determine a foolproof method to determine the sex of a bear before it is

The hunting of game species brings in millions of dollars to local, provincial, and state economies, some of which goes toward research and the purchase of bear habitat. The fact is, without regulated hunting, we would have fewer, not more, black bears.

shot. It has not proved to be an easy task. If you look at the hair around the bear's genitals when it is walking parallel to you, a female will have longer hairs protruding behind her vulva, while a male will have longer hairs protruding past his penis. These hairs generally protrude below the thigh when the bear is viewed from the side. This is, however, not a very satisfactory method of sexing bears in the field.

Every state and province where there are black bears offers a fall hunt. These are often combined with moose, caribou, or deer hunts. While fees for resident hunters are often quite low, non-resident hunters pay large sums for their licence and are often required to hire a guide as well. The economic value to a region for such hunts is substantial and quite important to the local economy.

Rifles, shot guns, old-fashioned smoothbore rifles, and bow and arrows are all used in the taking of bears. In many places there are separate seasons for each type of weapon.

Should bear hunting be allowed? To hunt a bear is a question of conscience, but regulated bear seasons do have their place. Most, but not all, bear researchers have no interest in hunting a bear, yet most support the need for this form of management. The revenue derived from hunting benefits the bears and other species— behavioral and ecological studies are financed, law enforcement to protect the species from poaching is increased, and suitable habitats are set aside and protected.

The argument is often made that funds can be found elsewhere to support these activities. However, as hunters and others point out, it is pressure from hunters and hunting organizations that have saved many of the game species that survive today. In the case of bears, the evidence is clear. The population is increasing, despite hunting, due to the management techniques employed to ensure a huntable bear population.

PART III: Getting Along in Bear Country

T he other parts of this book deal with the facts and figures I came across during my research and travels. It was my intention to provide a highly informative book about all facets of the black bear's life. But what I especially looked forward to communicating was people's direct, personal experiences with the bears, and the chapters in this part will, I hope, illuminate what

fascinating animals they are, and how we can learn to live safely with them as neighbours.

Black bears are not grizzlies—a fact all nature travellers should keep in mind. If you are planning to visit bear country, find out which species lives there. If you are travelling in an area occupied by both species, always give precedence to the grizzly bear "do's and don'ts" because grizzlies are far more aggres-

sive. If things get really dicey with a black bear, you still have a fairly good chance of getting out of the mess unhurt—with a grizzly, your chances aren't great.

The book *Bear Attacks: Their Causes and Avoidance,* by Stephen Herrero, is the best book I have come across about getting along with black and grizzly bears. As a professional photographer, it has helped me to overcome much of the fear I had about visiting bear country. Much of the advice that follows has been aided by Herrero's work as I offer my own interpretations and add some tips that I found worked for me. Herrero offers his advice from the perspective of someone who works in grizzly country. Serious bear-seekers should read his book.

26 The Tolerant Bear

When I was a teenager and dumps still existed in Algonquin Provincial Park in Ontario, I would take my dad's Brownie movie camera and hike around in the woods behind a dump, filming bears. Looking back, I now realize how foolish this was. There were 40 to 50 black bears frequenting the dump in those days, and I could usually find mothers with cubs, two-year-olds, and mature males. I had little knowledge of the dangers, and, in fact, the only book about black bears back then was *World of the Black Bear*, by Joe Van Wormer and it had just been published.

Ignorance was bliss. In all those hours of bear watching, I was never once threatened seriously. Knowing what I know now, though, I don't think I would take chances like that again. Who knew then that, two decades later, the

very park I prowled around would report the most number of fatal attacks by black bears in North America? It was the mid-1960s, before the horrific night of the grizzly attack in 1967 when two girls died in Glacier National Park in Montana. Back then, I believed bears to be dangerous, but not deadly. "Bear viewing" was a popular evening event—before the Glacier tragedy and the decision by U.S. parks to close their dumps.

Two of my early experiences remain etched in memory. On one occasion I was particularly bold and decided to go behind the dump to film the bears in a more natural setting. I spotted a few and sat down on a ridge to watch. A short distance away, on another ridge, I could see and hear other visitors, talking and laughing as they watched. One bear was walking

along the valley floor below, and I knew her. She was the one I called "Old Vee" because she sported a distinct "V" mark on her chest. The group (university students from Toronto) began tossing empty tins at her in order to see her run, and one hit its mark. What I learned since but didn't know then, is that when a bear is startled, it runs in the direction it is facing—and Old Vee was facing me!

She charged up the hill so fast that all I could do was remain quietly seated cross-legged. She stopped abruptly and sat down beside me, only an arm's length away. After making a popping sound with her teeth, she just looked at me. I smiled at her and we sat there together for a few minutes, listening to the yahoos on the other side laughing (though in their defence, they had no idea I was there). Then she stood, took a swipe at a sapling, and cut it in half. It fell on me, and she then rambled away, her dignity restored. I remained seated for a long while after, thankful and content.

I never saw Old Vee alive again. She was shot by park rangers two nights later along with about 30 other bears. In those days, once a bear got too used to people, it was destroyed. Less than a week later, new bears were scavenging the dump.

I have Old Vee's skull on my library shelf today. I found her body a few weeks after the incident—somebody else had already taken her canine teeth. Her skull serves as a reminder that "to feed a bear is to kill it."

The other incident happened a few years later, when a black bear charged me at a dump. I could have avoided the situation if I had backed off, but I was foolish. The bear growled from behind bushes several times, but I kept trying to get a picture. Then he charged, and I made it to the car just in time. My blurred photographs later revealed a recently injured bear. It took me a few years to get over that experience.

Encounters such as this one in Jasper National Park (Alberta) were common in the early 1970s throughout North America. It is remarkable that very few people were hurt. Education programs have all but put an end to this type of interaction.

Reflecting back, I'm not sure the bear really meant to harm me. Herrero makes the point that in national parks there are thousands of incidents without serious or even minor injuries occurring. Black bears, he says, are remarkably tolerant of people. Researcher Lynn Rogers' more recent work supports the same conclusion. Bears are followed for 24 hours at a time with no accompanying weapons—just experience—and no serious injury has resulted yet.

My experiences at the Vince Shute Wildlife Sanctuary (see Chapter 35) in northern Minnesota also gave me new respect and understanding of black bears. There, where Rogers took many of his photographs, I wandered among the bears, often at very close range. But I was always mindful that this was a special place. A year later while working with bears in Whistler, British Columbia, I did not assume they would act like the Shute bears (see Chapter 36). It takes time and experience before you begin to get a feel for their tolerance level.

Today most bear encounters are kept to a respectful distance between the two species. Most people know not to feed bears, and so bears learn to not view people as a source of treats.

I've seen a bear charge a crowd of onlookers in Great Smoky Mountains National Park without catching any of the fleeing tourists—it could have, but it didn't. I've seen people toss cans at bears without provoking a reaction. I've even watched a man pose his young daughter up against a feeding male to get a picture—the bear ignored them.

The point is that most black bears couldn't care less about getting close to people. They are not a threat to us, and given the chance, they'll run away or even go out of their way to avoid you long before you ever get near. The dangerous ones are rare and usually have been provoked or baited. The really dangerous ones—the ones that like to eat people—are rarer still. All said, there is little to fear from black bears when you enter their domain.

It takes time and experience before you begin to get a feel for their tolerance level.

27 Camping in Bear Country

Appendix III contains a list of places where bears can be spotted on a fairly regular basis. The list includes national, state, and provincial parks, and includes zoos, wildlife parks, and guided trips.

The vast majority of people who visit bear country will do so not with bear viewing in mind, but for a variety of other recreational purposes. If they see a bear, it may not add to their enjoyment of the trip, especially if the visitor sees it in a threatening situation. To avoid this, there are several things you can do.

Camp clean. A dirty campsite with garbage or food left lying about is an open invitation for bears or other nuisance wildlife to visit. This is especially true in parks where bears have learned to associate people with food, as was the case in the 1960s and early 1970s in the majority of parks across much of North America. The bears congregated around dumps, becoming habituated to the presence of people—a dangerous situation. The notion that animals in parks should live as natural a life as possible caught on across the country, and the dumps were closed.

The image of bear jams caused by habituated bears is still part of the public's popular perception of many parks. The question "Where are the bears?" is still frequently asked by tourists expecting to see a begging bear around the corner. The truth is that there are few, if any, parks left where black bears routinely beg for food. Bears that did persist in this habit after the dumps were closed were either relocated or killed.

Grizzly bears, it should be noted, never took to the begging-bear routine. That was the black bear's trick.

To avoid inviting a bear into camp, follow this advice:

- Don't camp near a bear trail or a seasonal feeding area such as a berry patch.
- Don't cook near your tent. A distance of one hundred metres or yards is recommended, but that is a luxury few campsites permit.
- Don't camp where food or garbage has been left. If you come across a campsite that has been left with food and empty tin cans littered about, consider moving on. Check the fire pit for unburned food as well. Even buried garbage may attract them.
- Don't camp where you find bear "signs" (droppings, tracks, markings).
- Don't sleep with food in your tent. Don't hide your food under a canoe—as if that flimsy wooden / fibreglass boat could stop a bear! A bear can easily smash a canoe and it can be a long walk (or swim) home.
- Don't store your food in a car with an open window.

○ **Dave Taylor: "Follow My Advice or …"**
The author describes two experiences that illustrate what happens if you fail to follow his "Don't" advice. "Once in Jasper National Park, Alberta, my wife and I awoke to find a black bear busily emptying a neighbouring camper's trunk. Another time, when we were in Yosemite National Park, California, we came across a car whose window had been ripped out to allow the bear access to the food stored in the trunk. The bear had climbed through the window, dragged the back seat into the front, and then pulled out the food, backpack and all."

So much for the "don'ts." Here is the "do" list.

- Do camp where you can store your food suspended from a tree, well away from camp. Again, one hundred metres (yards) is suggested. The food should be suspended at least twice the height of a man. (Never, ever hang the food over your tent!) If you can't find a suitable tree, then make sure your food is sealed in airtight containers.
- Do wash dishes thoroughly, and completely burn any waste food and tin cans with food remnants.
- Do pack your garbage out with you, including tin cans.
- Do consider a change of clothes if you've been cooking food with a strong odour, such as fish. Brook's Camp in Katmai National Park, Alaska, requires people on fishing trips to seal fish in zip-tight bags immediately after being caught. That's not a bad idea any place in bear country.
- Finally, one more "don't." Don't worry too much about bears. The chances of anything serious happening on your trip are very slim. The odds of you even seeing a bear aren't that great either, for that matter, unless you spend time looking for them.
- And one more "do." Do enjoy yourself!

○ A pair of novice campers kept food in their tent overnight in an Ontario park and woke up to the smell of bear breath in their tent. Worse, the bear was still there, feeding on the peanut butter!"

Black bears can be very bold when they learn people have food they like, but once they become a pest, they'll pay a high price for bad manners. The moral: to feed a bear is to kill it. Please keep your campsite clean!

This garbage can was supposed to be bear-proof. Apparently nobody told the bears that. Today, most parks have garbage containers that really are bear-proof, and waste management procedures have improved around towns, and regional dumps as well.

28 What To Do When You Meet a Black Bear

On one of my recent trips to Algonquin Provincial Park in Ontario, I was wandering down a portage trail tracking a moose I had just lost sight of when I heard the underbrush move. I stood very still, studying the location of the sound. Two black ears were all I could see. I waited for the bear to move—a two-year-old male emerged not 3 metres (10 feet) from me. I took its picture, it ran away at the sound, and I began breathing again.

What do you do if you meet a black bear? If you see the bear ambling down an old road some distance from you, make a loud noise so it knows you are there. Generally, that is enough to make it disappear. What if you stumble on one at close range while you're berry picking or hiking? You can still try yelling, but I would suggest the following tactics that have all worked for me one time or another.

- *Never run from it.* Running from a predator triggers the attack response. It's an invitation to play tag, and you can't outrun a bear in the woods.
- *Always face the bear.* Most predators are reluctant to attack an opponent head-on. I have no idea why this works, but it generally does. Perhaps predators like the element of surprise.
- *Talk to the bear—quietly.* Let it know you are there. You can try yelling if it approaches you, but in my experience with various big game animals, including moose, elk, bison, and grizzly bears, the quiet approach generally works well, especially when combined with the next suggestion.
- *Back up slowly, but always keep your eyes on the bear.* There is, in wildlife behaviour studies, a concept known as "flight or fight." Black bears, more than grizzlies, prefer flight—running away—so if the bear thinks you are far enough away from it that it has the option of vanishing into the woods, it will.

But what if the bear doesn't turn and run? First you decide if it is a bear familiar with people or a predatory bear that has designs on you for dinner. This second type is discussed in Chapter 29, Killer Bears. If you run into a habituated bear, it will likely have a series of bluffs that are designed to scare you—and they will! It may stomp its feet loudly. It may huff or snort at you. It may make a popping sound. Or it might flat out charge you! None of these actions are generally associated with a predatory bear that is looking at you as its next meal. Keep cool and don't run! Yelling at or chasing the bear might work to scare it off only if it hasn't experienced this human response too many times before.

Keep cool and don't run!

~

What about playing dead?

What about playing dead? According to Herrero, that depends on the situation. Close to 95 percent of recorded bear "attacks" occur near campsites, picnic areas, roadsides (where the bear is begging), or at garbage dumps—where the bear was most likely after food or felt crowded when the "attack" happened. Playing dead won't work because most of these aggressive moves are designed to either scare you away from the food or to get you out of the way so the bear can retreat. Again, back away to give it space, and let it have the food if you're carrying any. Herrero suggests that playing dead is only of value if the bear views you as a threat, as a mother with cubs would.

On the trail, away from those areas where typical habituated bear encounters occur, the steps outlined above work best.

What should you do if a bear approaches your picnic site? Usually a bit of yelling and waving your hands will do, but if not, retreat, keeping your eyes on the bear.

○ In extreme circumstances, the bear may come to within millimetres (less than an inch) of you. George Kolenosky, a leading Ontario bear researcher, tells of an incident that occurred when he was live-trapping bears for radio collaring. He had caught a cub and was holding it when the mother charged full tilt out of the bush. Kolenosky carried a handgun that day and could have shot her, but he stood his ground. She stopped inches away, her nose near his boot. For long seconds, they stood staring at each other— then she moved away. He finished with the cub and released it. No harm done.

Playing dead is only of value if the bear views you as a threat, as a mother with cubs would.

A stressed bear will sometimes lower its head, pop its teeth, and even stamp the ground with its front feet. This means you are too close, and the bear is deciding whether to fight or flee. If it decides on fight, it will probably cause some injury, but it will not eat you! All it wants to do is get rid of the threat.

29 Killer Bears

The footage was riveting. Although shown on one of those home video programs that play on Sunday evenings, it wasn't funny—the video camera operator was being stalked by a black bear! The man had wandered up a stream to go fishing when he encountered an average size bear while his buddies were off in another part of the lake. The video captured classic bear behaviour when it sets its mind on dining on human flesh. There was no bluff charge, no popping of teeth, no snorting. The man stood his ground, yelling at the bear, but to no effect. It just came forward, slowly and deliberately.

It didn't press its attack, but it didn't back off. This might have been because the man kept facing the bear while, incredibly, continuing to tape the incident. The sound recording eerily captured the increasing panic in the man's voice. He did manage to escape, barely, by wading into the chest deep water of the stream. The bear retreated at this point, only to return seconds later to make one final attempt. Then it left for good.

Tragically, in May of 1978 a group of teenage boys fishing in Algonquin Provincial Park in Ontario were not so lucky. Three of the four boys were killed, two of them after being stalked, and all three were partially fed on. The fourth boy went for help when he couldn't find his friends. The bear, a healthy male, was killed a few days later as it stalked its hunters. Although many theories to explain the killings were put forward, ranging from a mad bear to the smell of fish on the boys, the general conclusion was that it was a clear case of predation.

On October 11, 1991, a couple arrived to camp on Bate's Island in Lake Opeongo, one of the largest and most accessible lakes in Algonquin Provincial Park. Investigators later pieced together the tragedy from the evidence they found. The attack occurred when the two were setting up camp. The woman was attacked first. Her companion tried to drive the bear off with an oar, hitting the bear with it until the oar broke. The bear then killed the man—a single blow to the head killed both. The bear dragged the bodies away, and fed on them over the next five days.

When the Ministry of Natural Resources searched the area they found the corpses under a pile of leaves. The bear was shot, and an autopsy determined that the bear was a healthy, eight-year-old-male with no abnormalities. Evidence at the site also indicated that the couple did nothing wrong. Their campsite was clean, and although there was food in the frying pan, the bear had not touched it.

More important, they did the right thing when they confronted the bear. Although with most bears a quiet retreat or standing your ground works fine, with a bear bent on eating you, there are two choices: run for safety—a tree, the water, or some shelter—or stand and fight. If the latter is your only option, be as aggressive and loud as possible. Grab a log! Throw stones! Charge the bear!

All of these incidents appear to be deliberate cases of a large predator (mostly males) selecting humans as its next source of protein. An average of one person per year has met the same fate across North America. Most of the killings have occurred in the northern half of the continent in wilderness areas, outside of national, state, or provincial parks. There have also been several injuries and near misses. The evidence supports the theory that these healthy, otherwise normal bears have likely had no experience with people, and when they stumble across them, they react as they would to any other potential prey species.

Of the 20 people killed by bears that Stephen Herrero documents in his book *Bear Attacks: Their Causes and Avoidance*, half of the victims were under the age of 18, and 5 were under 10 years old. Size matters, and a bear is less likely to attack something they perceive as being bigger than they. It is a natural animal response to stand or rear up in the face of danger—an attempt to intimidate the predator. Therefore in bear country, children, especially infants, should be watched with great care. If threatened by a predator bear, don't crouch or bend down. Make yourself appear as tall as you can by raising your hands above your head.

○ Recognizing a "Killer" Bear

How do you know if the black bear you meet wants you as the main course? The odds are that any bear you meet will be a "normal" bear (see Chapter 28, What To Do When You Meet a Black Bear). With "killer" bears, the animal's approach will be deliberate, without growls or bluff charges. If you yell at it or back away, it will just keep walking toward you, and you will know then that it is acting different from a panhandling or curious one.

Algonquin Park has had five reported bear fatalities since it was created in 1893. There is one other possibility—a farmer (farming was allowed in the park in the early days) may have died at the paws of a bear or from natural causes and simply been dined on. Since the 1978 killings, over 8,000,000 visitors have visited the park, and the vast majority never sees a black bear. For those that do, the experience is usually limited to a brief glimpse of an animal vanishing into the woods. It is trite, but true, that you are in more danger driving to work than you are from any type of bear attack—black, polar, or grizzly.

There is, on average, less than one person killed by a black bear per year in North America. Prior to the first Algonquin killings in 1978, there were only 11 recorded deaths in all of the 1900s. Less than one in 870,000 black bears living in the woods is likely in any given year to prey on a person. When you factor in the number of people venturing into bear country or living close to it, the odds are astronomically against being preyed upon.

If you look at the numbers, rather than asking why black bears prey on humans, the question really is why more black bears don't? Again, there is no simple answer. Why a few should behave differently remains a mystery.

An Atypical Attack — The Mary Beth Miller Tragedy

In the summer of 2000, Mary Beth Miller, 24, a bronze medallist at the North American biathlon championships, tragically died from a black bear attack. Miller, who was from Yellowknife in the Northwest Territories, was in training at Canadian Forces Base Valcartier when the attack occurred in early July. The base, located northwest of Quebec City, is home to the Myriam Bedard Biathlon Centre, where athletes train for university and Olympic competition. Miller went running by herself that Sunday morning at about 9 a.m., ignoring posted signs not to enter the wooded track area alone. Bears were known to be in the area, and a warning had been posted after one had chased a group of cyclists a few weeks before.

About 11 a.m. her coach noticed she was missing and alerted the military police. They found her body about 800 metres (875 yards) from the road. There were bear teeth and claw marks on her head and neck, and she had been dragged some distance. While an autopsy was performed on

Miller, wildlife officials set traps, and a 75-kilogram (165-pound) female was caught near where the killing had taken place. Its size and the spacing of its teeth matched the runner's wounds perfectly, and the bear was destroyed.

The attack was not "typical." It did not involve a male bear, the victim was not eaten, and it took place in an area where bears would be familiar with people. The sow's teats were full of milk, suggesting she had cubs in the area. A subsequent search however, found no sign of cubs and led to speculation that they had been killed. Their death, it was thought, might have caused the bear to become aggressive and attack the runner. Perhaps she was highly agitated because they had disappeared. Maybe she just attacked to avenge the death of her cubs.

○ Having People for Dinner

Black bears are one of the few land animals in North America known to actually eat humans. The bull walrus and the polar bear have also attacked and eaten people. Surprisingly, grizzly bears almost never feed on humans after they have killed them—their attack is strictly defensive. There has only been one reported case of a wolf eating a person (in Saskatchewan in late 2005) and only a very few attacks.

In over 40 years of watching and photographing bears, this was the only one that I think ever meant me harm. It had just been in a fight with another bear, and I did what you are never supposed to do—I continued to approach it after it repeatedly growled at me to stay away. It just wanted space and it certainly did not see me as prey.

Bison

Orca

Grey wolf

Walrus

Elk

Grizzly

Which of these animals do you think injure the most number of people in western national parks? Answer: Elk are the most dangerous, and bison injure more people than black bears and grizzlies combined. Even white-tailed deer and moose have a worse record than do black bears. Why? People are foolish—they think these animals are cute domestic animals. They are wrong.

30 Black Bear Viewing at Its Best

Where are the best places to view and photograph black bears? There are lots of places to look, but few that can guarantee success. Although the black bear is the most common and widespread of North America's three species, it is, by virtue of its habitat, the most difficult to see. There are many excellent places in Alaska to view and photograph grizzly bears. Churchill, Manitoba, offers virtually guaranteed polar bear viewing in the fall. But these places are relatively open areas, where the bears live and feel safe. Black bears prefer forests, hidden from view. Actually, the best way to see wild black bears is to hire a guide.

So where to go? For areas and specific locations, see Appendix III, which provides a list of good viewing lodges and tours, and has a rated list of parks, preserves, and sanctuaries to visit. The places in this chapter have proved some of the best bear-viewing opportunities available.

The very best place to view wild, free-roaming black bears in all of North America is The American Bear Association's **Vince Shute Wildlife Sanctuary** in Minnesota (see Chapter 35). Some, though, will find it a slightly artificial experience because viewers are limited both in time and area where they can see the bears.

The best park in the eastern United States is **Great Smoky Mountains National Park**. There are between four and six hundred bears, and many meadows and clearings that the bears frequent. Cade's Cove at the south end of the park is an excellent place for sightings, and you'll also see white-tailed deer, wild turkeys, and other wildlife. The bears are quite used to people, and a few may still try begging. Remember that feeding a bear is against the law and may result in the bear being destroyed.

In 1991 the park began experimenting with captured panhandlers by "working-up" and then releasing them back into the area where they were caught. They were subjected to a thorough medical examine that, while harmless, was unpleasant for the bear. The hope is that they will once again learn to fear people.

Also in the east, New York's **Adirondack State Park** has provided good bear viewing in recent years, and Pennsylvania's Pocono Mountains are worth a visit.

In the west, **Yellowstone National Park** has a large number of bears, though you have a better chance of seeing a grizzly there these days. The same applies to **Glacier National Park** in Montana. However, a visit in the spring to any national or state park where bears are common will likely present viewing opportunities as the bears feed on the green-up.

Yosemite National Park in California has a good black bear population. In the 1970s some of these bears became quite adept at "mugging" hikers, but most of this type of behaviour has been cleaned up. **Redwood** and **Sequoia National Parks** are also good locations to try.

In Canada, several of the mountain parks in Alberta and British Columbia offer good black bear opportunities. Good bets are **Waterton Lakes**, **Banff**, and **Jasper National Parks** in Alberta and **Glacier**, **Revelstoke**, **Kootenay**, **Pacific Rim**, and **Yoho** in British Columbia. Spring provides the best viewing opportunities from the road, as bears will be out feeding on the green-up in valleys. By summer they move to the high country, away from the roads.

Riding Mountain National Park in Manitoba and **Prince Albert National Park** in Saskatchewan both have some good opportunities. Again, spring is best, but in Riding Mountain National Park bears are attracted to the fall mast on the oak trees on the eastern side of the park.

Tofino and **Ucluelet** on Vancouver Island both have bears on the exposed tidal flats. On one trip alone I saw four black bears, a dozen seals, and one wolf. **Whistler**, known for its skiing, (see Chapter 36) has developed a bear-viewing operation, and bears are frequently seen from the gondolas on both Whistler and Blackcomb Mountains. You can also see bears while just driving the roads in this area.

Knight Inlet is known for its grizzly and black bears, as well as orcas and bald eagles. **Terrace** offers a chance to see the white-phase Kermode's bears, and if you are adventurous, you can take a trip to Princess Royal Island, where Adventure Canada offers a wildlife tour to see these white-phase bears, as well as killer whales and sea lions.

In southeast Alaska, **Annan Creek** near **Wrangell** offers good black bear viewing in July and August. The bears are feeding on salmon and you may even see a grizzly.

The inexperienced wildlife photographer should never get this close to a bear. There are lots of places you can safely view black bears without putting yourself at risk.

Black bears frequent trails, and hikers should always keep an eye out for them. This one was photographed on Whistler Mountain from a helicopter.

Viewing at low tide from the safety of a tour boat can be an exciting adventure along both coasts.

31 The Black Bears of Waterton Lakes

My brother-in-law, Jim Markou, and I took a three-week trip to Montana and Wyoming one summer, photographing wildlife. Bears were, of course, ever on our mind, but other than in controlled environments, we had succeeded in photographing a grand total of zero in the wild. We ended up, however, with a picture perfect ending to our trip.

It was time to head home, and we decided at the last minute to revisit Waterton Lakes National Park in Alberta on our way back to Calgary. Our intention was to take more photographs of some trophy-sized mule deer bucks we'd seen a few weeks earlier. At the entrance station we asked about them. The ranger, a young college student, replied she hadn't seen the bucks for a few days, but when we asked about bears, she replied, "Oh, they're all over the place. You'll see them right from this road."

We thanked her and drove off. "Typical ranger," Jim mocked. We'd met this type in every park we visited—summertime employees who gave pat answers to the tourists to keep them happy. Sure, there were bear sightings every now and then, but they were chance encounters, few and far between, and the bears would disappear quickly. We had once sat for eight hours at one of the gateways in Yellowstone where grizzlies were seen "regularly." We saw marmots, moose, and deer but no bears. This visit to Waterton was not likely to yield anything much different.

Then, to our great delight, we spotted a bear running across the open meadow below us—and less than five minutes after entering the park! Two hours and eight or nine bears

later, I much regretted my initial reaction to the student ranger. She was right! Black bears were everywhere—feeding on berries, running across meadows, and playing with their cubs. At times the bears were less than two metres (six feet) away from us. This was not by design—we were busy shooting a bear on the other side of the road when another rambled up close from behind.

It was a wonderful day, and the only annoying event was the arrival of a park warden. A

crowd had gathered and was watching a sow and two cubs on a small rise above the road. The warden watched for about 10 minutes and then, through his loudspeaker, told people to move on. He then blew on his siren to scare the bears off. We came back five minutes later to find the warden still patrolling the area. We left again, to photograph in another area where we had spotted a bear.

When we returned the warden was gone and so, apparently, were the bears, but it only took us a few minutes to find them again. As it turned out, we had them for the most part to ourselves for almost two hours. Other people did arrive, but they seldom spent long watching the bears, and not once did I see anyone attempt to feed them. This was in sharp contrast to my experience 20 years before when my wife and I honeymooned in Yellowstone. In those days black bears were everywhere on the road and feeding was common. People's attitudes, I learned, had changed.

Our adventure at Waterton Lakes that afternoon fed my desire to write this book. For the next 10 years (and counting) I continued my study of bears, their researchers, and their natural habitat.

Black bears were everywhere, feeding on berries, running across meadows, and playing with their cubs.

Waterton offers a great variety of habitats for bears to thrive in. Other national, provincial, and state parks offer bear-viewing opportunities, but this one day was exceptional.

32 Two Winter Days in the Life of a Bear Researcher

Chapleau, Ontario, lies about 800 kilometres (500 miles) north of Toronto in the boreal forest. It is a small town whose main industry is logging. It also happens to be on the border of the world's largest game preserve (Chapleau Crown Game Preserve), where moose, wolf, lynx, and black bear abound.

Twice a year the predator biologist Dr. Martyn Obbard brings a crew of Ontario Ministry of Natural Resources (MNR) personnel to this preserve to continue a black bear study begun in 1988. There are three study groups—one inside the game preserve that is not hunted and two outside the preserve that are. I was kindly invited to join the team for two days on their winter denning study in early March, and it turned out to be one of my most interesting experiences with bears.

I arrived with Don McClement, a fellow photographer / naturalist, and it was his nephew, Mike Buckner, a conservation officer and volunteer to the study, who first suggested that I contact the MNR about participating. Dr. Obbard had 47 radio-collared bears to visit in their dens and had set aside two weeks for the task.

The core group of researchers would be divided into three teams led by Dr. Obbard, Anita Schenk (black bear technologist), and Tim Moody (Chapleau conservation officer). The group also included Lucy Brown, a predator biologist; Ian Salisbury, who was there on a six-week university placement from England; and Dr. Obbard's son, Jeff.

The group had been busy preparing gear and snow machines so that when the 20 MNR volunteers arrived late the next day, the work could get into full swing. They had examined their first bear of the season the day we arrived. Sunday would be the second trial run. We were given a room and told to be up by 6:30 a.m.

Day 1

Sunday morning did not present ideal conditions. Snow had begun falling during the night and would not stop all day. The temperature hovered about -30° Celsius (-22° Fahrenheit). By 8:30 the decision was made to go, but some of the snow machines were uncooperative. After being coaxed into life—a bone-chilling operation with tinkering required *sans*-gloves—we headed off.

In the fall, Martyn, Anita, and Lucy had radio-tracked each bear to its den and flagged the location so they would be relatively easy to find in winter. "Relatively easy" meant up to an hour (and in some cases more) on snowmobiles in soft, powdery snow and then a short hike on snowshoes, with some up to a kilometre or two. The snow machines would often get stuck in deep snow and have to be lifted or dragged out. Snowshoe trails had to be created through often-heavy bush and usually up hills. And all this with 20 kilogram (44 pound) backpacks loaded with radio telemetry equipment, assorted drugs, nets, shovels, scales, ropes, and calipers, as well as lunch and a thermos of hot coffee or tea.

And after all this, the real work began.

Naively, I thought we would do four or five bears per day. As it turned out, one was a full day's work, maybe two if things went really smoothly. Our first encounter was highly unusual, while our second, the next day, more typical.

The first bear was a "runner." Dr. Obbard had just opened up the den entrance when the female's head appeared. The team knew what was coming and quickly tried to close off the bear's exit by blocking it with shovels and snowshoes. This sow would have none of that and came barreling out. Anita tried to tackle it, but it was too little too late. "Follow her and try and to tree her!" Martyn barked.

We watched as the bear vanished into the forest with Anita struggling gamely along behind. Our immediate concern was that her cubs would follow her. Martyn quickly squeezed his head into the den and shone a flashlight. He knew she had three cubs in the fall, and as far as he could see, two or three were there.

Leaving Tim to watch the den, we went off to try and dart her.

Darting in this situation is done with a hypodermic needle that is mounted on the end of a plunge stick. Darting guns are not used because the den site and the deep snow allow the researchers to get quite close to the bear. The problem is that the liquid drug freezes and has to be warmed by hand, even though a heated thermos is brought along for that purpose. The thermos, however, can only be used to keep the drugs warm at a distance. When the actual darting takes place, the needle needs to be at hand. It is then that it freezes.

One cub did try and make a break for it, and Tim fell on it, jabbing it with a dose of the drug. Yearlings are tough to sedate, and this one was really scrappy. The cub would be number 550, and it would wear a radio collar for the next year or so. As part of the design, it would fall off when the bear grew to a certain point. The bear weighed in at 22.5 kilograms (45 pounds).

Dr. Obbard had returned by now after getting half a dose into the sow before she moved farther up a fir tree and out of reach. The main concern at this point was to keep the cub warm.

The cold temperature and falling snow was a problem, so the cub was dealt with as quickly as possible. I was impressed throughout my experience with the concern shown for each bear's welfare. During the entire course of the study, only a very few have been lost. On two occasions in the past, mouth-to-mouth resuscitation was actually administered and in one case was successful.

Number 550 was returned to the den and tucked safely in. Anita stood guard while the rest of us went to collect its mother, number 009. We never did get the other cubs out of the den because we were unable to reach them. The den had a section that Dr. Obbard was unable to reach into but into which the cub managed to squeeze itself.

Originally collared in 1989, number 009 was well known to Martyn. She was eight or nine years old and this was her second litter. She'd had two cubs in her first litter—one of those, a daughter, was denned not too far away. Typical of black bears, she was sharing a portion of her mother's range. The fact is that very few of the cubs here reach maturity. Male bears take most. We hoped 550 would be an exception to the rule.

Meanwhile, 009 was waiting in the fir tree, very much awake, and well out of our reach. The only way to get her was to chop down the tree, a drastic measure rarely required. The concern was that she would not return to her yearlings, and den up someplace else. The youngsters would not have the benefit of her warmth for the rest of the winter, and if they were on their own come spring, they would have a poorer chance of survival.

Within minutes the tree and the bear were down. The deep snow padded the bear's landing and slowed her escape. As soon as she hit the ground the crew was on her, and a full dose of tranquilizer was administered. She was then let go and passed out about 15 metres (50 feet) from her crash point.

The bear suffered only one scratch from her adventure. She was lifted onto a tarp and dragged back near the den, a few hundred metres (yards) away, where she was then "worked up." She weighed 55.6 kilograms (122.5 pounds). At about 3:00 p.m. we slid her back into her den, and by 4:30 we were back at the camp.

Clockwise This mother bear was wide awake and burst out of the den before anyone could stop her.

She scrambled up a tree but could not be left there because there was concern she wouldn't return to her cubs.

The tree had to come down with the bear—it was a soft landing.

Dr. Obbard rushed in to quickly administer another tranquilizer shot.

That night, an additional dozen MNR personnel arrived to join the three teams. While all were salaried, work on this project was strictly on a volunteer basis. Most of their regular jobs were as biologists, foresters, technicians, or conservation officers, and they would have to make up the time lost from their regular jobs when they got back. But nobody minded—they were there for the experience of working with the bears.

Day 2

The second day dawned bright and sunny, although the temperature would hardly rise above -20° Celsius (-4° Farenheit.). With the weather more cooperative and the additional hands, preparations went smoothly, and by 9:00 a.m. the three crews were all on their way. The sun lent a feeling of warmth to the day, and the trip in was not as strenuous as the day before. Once again I was with Martyn and Lucy. Martyn's son Jeff accompanied us, along with Gary Parker and Tom Nash, both from the northern Ontario town of Atikokan. Gary and Tom had participated the year before and had enjoyed it so much they had come back for more.

The bears were also more cooperative, and within minutes of finding the den the sow was drugged. Martyn and Gary gave her 10 minutes to go under, then dragged her out and carried her to the tarp that was spread out to keep her off the snow.

Reading her weight was the first order of business. Tom cut down a sturdy young tree to hook the net onto. Each end of the tree rested on two people's shoulders, who then hoisted the pole with the bear slung beneath. She was exactly the same weight as the one the previous day— 55.6 kilograms (122.5 pounds). We then measured her chest girth, contour (tip of the nose to the second tail vertebrae), fat pinch, neck size, skull width, the distance between her eyes, and the length of her humerus and ulna.

Her foot pads were also checked. Bears shed the soles of their feet and replace them with new skin. The state of this shedding is one way of gauging their health in the den. They also assessed her condition by examining the quality of her hair and fur. On a scale from 1 to 5, with 5 being the best and achieved in late fall, she was rated a 2, which isn't too bad for a March bear. I could feel her ribs, so she was thin. A rating of 1 means the bear is in critical shape. A rating of 3 means she is in excellent shape for a winter bear.

The paws are checked to see if new pads have started to grow. Bears replace their old pads each winter.

This bear was number 017 and she was trapped in 1989. Last winter she had two cubs of her own, and Martyn had added another by bringing it to her den when she was worked up. We were delighted to discover that she had accepted it, for there were three cubs with her. She was also in need of another radio collar so her old one was stripped off and then replaced.

○ Throughout the procedure, the bears' eyes are covered to prevent retinal damage. The drug that is given makes the bears go limp, but they are not unconscious, and their eyes are open and fully dilated. When photographing in the den, the use of a flash is allowed only if the eyes are covered.

Then it was the cubs' turn. Martyn slid into the den on his back. When you are in this position it is almost impossible to get any leverage, and you rely on the people outside to grab and pull you out. Martyn's signal for this was the tapping of his boot heels together.

He hadn't been in more than a few seconds when his heels did more than tap—they flailed wildly. As he was pulled out, we could hear a muffled yell from within. Not sure whether he had yelled to stop, the others stopped pulling, but then the "ow!" and "pull!" were clear, and he was tugged out within seconds. The third cub, which had not been drugged, had chewed at his hand (no damage done) and swiped at his head (a small scratch).

After a brief rest he went back in and grabbed the sleeping cub, and Gary was soon able to drug the third. At this point I asked if I might be able to retrieve the final cub. After

being assured that it was sedated, I squeezed in—well tried to. I had to remove my outer jacket, my photo vest, and my snowmobile coat before I could wedge inside the narrow opening. A full-grown bear had come out through this!

Number 603 lay just out of reach, and I squirmed in a bit farther. The den did not smell at all, and it was surprisingly small, certainly not enough room for me to turn around in. The bottom was covered with leaves and other forest debris the mother had dragged in last fall. The walls were smooth except where roots dangled free of soil. I reached out and grabbed 603's rump and tugged. "Pull," I yelled, and in a few seconds the cub and I were out of the den.

The next step was to give the sow the antidote and return her to the den. Each cub was then examined and the same data recorded. In addition, old ear tags were removed and new, larger ones attached. Each yearling was also fitted with a radio collar that would allow researchers to study what would happen to them in the months to come.

When the cubs were returned to the den, mom was starting to come around, so the den was quickly re-covered with pine boughs and snow. Three hours had passed.

Meanwhile, Don's team had checked a sow that was supposed to have yearlings, but they had apparently been killed early in the spring, because she had bred again, producing a single newborn cub. This was a rarity that year, as most sows had yearlings like I had seen. I very much regretted not seeing a newborn, but that just gave me reason to return—something I fully intend to do.

We left that evening to go back to our regular jobs in the city, filled with admiration for the work these men and women do and a deeper understanding of the black bear's winter life.

The author holding a cub he had just pulled out of the den.

The team weighs a cub, and it is quickly returned to its mother. Although this interference with the bear's denning is intrusive, such research gives us a better understanding of the bear's needs, and the species as a whole will benefit from it. Note the injury to Dr. Obbard's scalp from his experience retrieving the cub. Its yet-to-be-sedated sibling was defending the den!

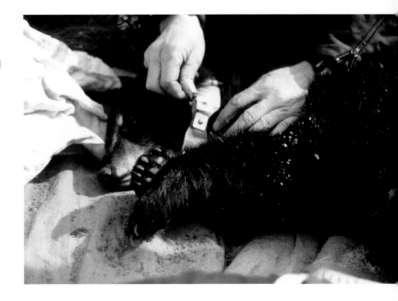

A cub is fitted with a radio collar. The cloth covering its eyes had to be removed but was quickly put back after the fitting.

33 Summertime Research

We were standing in what Dr. Obbard called very good bear country. Although the forest had been clear-cut, this patch of the Chapleau Crown Game Reserve had been logged with wildlife in mind. I could see for miles across the gently rolling terrain. Here and there stands of uncut spruce trees or aspens punctuated the horizon. The ground was covered with low green growth: new trees, blueberry bushes, and fireweed. It offered lots of food for bears in the form of summer berries. A boreal forest offers very little to bears unless there are meadows or patches of burned-over ground. The forest cover prevents sunlight from reaching the forest floor, and berries need lots of sunlight to grow. The loggers had essentially opened up the forest.

But bears need cover too to escape the heat and predators, and sufficient stands of uncut forest had been left to provide shelter for bears, moose, and other wildlife.

It was a fine July day, and I had returned to the Chapleau area to observe summer field research. This consists of trapping bears and then fitting them with radio collars. We were on our way to check the traps, all located in stands of trees. Orange ribbons marked their location.

The traps consisted of two or three large steel drums welded together. A spring-loaded gate was at one end and at the other end was a small platform that, when disturbed by the bear, would trigger the gate to fall. Fresh meat had been placed on the platform.

The traps worked very well, and a number of bears had been caught that season. Because bears are largely territorial, unknown bears were unlikely to be found this late in the study. Research was in its fourth summer, and virtually all the bears had been collared. Still, there was work to do. Batteries had to be changed, collars repaired, and new data recorded. How much weight had the bear gained or lost since last summer? Did it have cubs? Had it grown longer? How healthy was it?

At least once each summer, a bear would be worked up. It would be tranquilized, dragged out of the trap, weighed, and its length and

This bear had been worked up a few weeks earlier, so was simply released. It had returned for a good meal.

This bear, previously collared, is tranquilized after entering the trap.

girth recorded. Blood would be taken, and if it was lactating, a sample of its milk might be drawn for analysis. If it was a female with cubs, an attempt would be made to locate the cubs. They were often found up a nearby tree, but if the team couldn't locate them, there was little worry—within an hour or so the cubs would be reunited with their mother.

Some of the bears take a real liking to the trap. Many are captured several times through the summer months and are released with little ceremony. The trap is opened and the bear walks or runs out. Apparently the free meal is worth the wait for freedom.

Most bears in the study wear radio collars that are monitored daily. A researcher drives the logging roads, using a directional antenna to locate individual bears. Each bear broadcasts on a specific frequency. It takes two readings to locate a bear and the readings must be taken several kilometres (miles) apart. With over one hundred bears radio-collared, it takes awhile to locate them all, and every now and then a bear (usually a male) wanders out of range. When this happens the bears can sometimes be located from a plane using the same technique.

The team works up the bear, taking various measurements.

The bear is weighed and then given another shot to counteract the sedative.

The radio collar does not seem to bother the bears much, and it transmits a signal so that it can be located.

A few of the bears wear Global Positioning System (GPS) collars. Larger mammals such as moose and elk have been studied using GPS for some time, but these collars weigh about 2 kilograms (4.5 pounds), and Dr. Obbard felt the weight was too much for the smaller bears to carry. He had approached Lotek, a company that designs, among other things, remote wildlife monitoring systems, to develop a light-weight model, and it was working well.

GPS collars provide a more detailed view of the bears' travels than do regular radio-collars. The information can be stored on a computer and does not require a researcher to be in the field. Data can be collected in the lab.

○ GPS Collars

GPS technology consists of three parts: satellites, ground receivers, and hand-held or mounted units. There are 24 satellites orbiting Earth at 11,000 nautical miles. Each orbits Earth in 12 hours. They send back data that is received by ground receivers. To get an accurate reading, at least six satellite signals must be received. This will give the researcher the location (longitude and latitude) and altitude of its subject with an accuracy of within one metre (yard). Three satellites were sufficient for the Chapleau study's needs.

Technicians in the field monitor the location of bears and record their findings on a map. They seldom actually see the bears.

34 Bear With Us: A Labour of Love

Harmony climbed up Mike as if she were climbing a tree and began nuzzling his neck. With a sigh, Mike sat down, giving in to youngster. But this was not your everyday cuddling between parent and child. This was a six-month-old bear cub treating a man as if it were her mother.

Harmony and Mike McIntosh have a rather special relationship, but it is not one that Mike had hoped for. He would much rather have never met the cub, preferring, instead, for her to have remained in the wild. But circumstances had conspired against them.

> ## Mike picked up the three-kilogram (seven-pound) orphaned cub and took her home. She wasn't his first, and she wouldn't be his last.

Mike had received a phone call on April 30 of that year. A man had reported a small bear cub bawling for help in front of his cottage, and Mike went out to collect it. Although the snow had melted in most of the woods, the small pond was still ice-covered, and there in the middle of it sat this very small, unhappy, black creature. He presumed her mother was a victim of the spring bear hunt. Mike picked up the three-kilogram (seven-pound) orphaned cub and took her home. She wasn't his first, and she wouldn't be his last.

Mike began working with bears when he volunteered at an Ontario wildlife rehabilitation centre, the Aspen Valley Sanctuary run by Audrey Tourney. He became so involved that he decided to quit his job in the city to be closer to wildlife. He moved up to the Huntsville area of Ontario, and in 1992 established and continues to run a sanctuary devoted to black bears called Bear With Us. He supports himself by working in town as the manager of a car dealership, but most of his spare time and money goes to the bears.

○ **Bear With Us** provides many different services. Mike responds to nuisance bear calls and has helped resolve conflicts without injury to either bears or people. He also provides public education about the need to improve how people dispose of garbage or compost. Bear With Us also provides rehabilitation for orphan cubs and injured bears, and offers permanent sanctuary for non-releasable adults, such as abused circus bears.

A captured adult bear is seldom kept for long. Once assured that it is healthy, Mike takes the bear to a safe area and releases it. However, most of the bears that come his way are cubs. When I visited Mike in July he had 15 bears under his care, and all but two were cubs-of-the-year. Earlier that summer he had 31. He is so well known for his innovative methods of reintroducing cubs into the wild that many of the bears come from outside Ontario. That summer he had received 12 from Manitoba.

Besides working with the bears, Mike also advises other bear rehabilitators on how to best prepare cubs for release back into the wild. He has received calls from Arkansas, British Columbia, Florida, North Carolina, and Texas.

So what exactly does Mike do? If he gets a cub as young as Harmony, he usually begins by raising it in his house. He has to feed the cub every three hours, and that poses a problem. He and his assistant both work during the day, so they reverse the cub's timetable. It sleeps during the day and is fed at night. Harmony never took to the bottle though; she preferred to lap her milk out of a bowl.

In order to get some sleep, Mike often ended up sleeping with Harmony. She'd cuddle up and then start sucking on his neck, not for food but for comfort. It was a behaviour that continued for several months. She produced what he describes as a "happy chuckle" as she moves her tiny mouth around his neck. This is the same sound that I've heard nursing wild cubs make.

Boo, a cub that arrived in late August, hadn't learned this trick. He sucked on his own toes when he finished eating or playing, but it seemed to serve the same purpose. Mike thinks that Boo missed out on some basic contact needs when he was young. Boo came to Mike from Detroit. The Michigan Anti-Cruelty Society had rescued the cub from its owner, and Mike agreed to take it with the understanding that he could, if necessary, return him to the wilds in Michigan.

Mike took Harmony and Boo on walks to show them what to eat. Not all of his cubs are this habituated. Harmony and Boo had taken to Mike, but the Manitoba cubs avoided him and could not be trusted to stay with him on a walk in the woods. Like a mother bear, Mike sometimes had to scold Harmony when she got too playful. At times she required a firm cuff, but often a sharp "no" sufficed.

On my first walk with Mike and Harmony, she tasted blueberries for the first time. That was in July. By October she was finishing off the last of the wild crop, and Boo was eating them too. For the captured cubs that are too nervous or traumatized to join Mike on his walks, he pulls complete plants from the berry patches and brings them back for them to feed on in their cages.

> For the captured cubs that are too nervous or traumatized to join Mike on his walks, he pulls complete plants from the berry patches and brings them back for them to feed on in their cages.

He never feeds the bears people food, such as donuts. He doesn't want them to develop a taste for food that could get them into trouble. A local resort donates salmon and other left over foods, and the Ministry of Natural Resources supports him by bringing in the occasional road-killed animal. Still, it costs Mike about three hundred dollars a week in the summer to feed the bears. Some of this he gets from donations, but most of it comes from his own pocket. A Canadian airline donated free flights to bring the young cubs to Ontario from Manitoba.

By October Mike releases most of his cubs back into the wild. Release sites must meet three criteria: they must offer plenty of natural bear food, they must be relatively remote from towns and provincial parks, and preferably, they must have no hunting allowed. That summer only Harmony and Boo would hibernate in a den created for them on Mike's property. Boo now weighed 34 kilograms (75 pounds) and Harmony about 30 kilograms (65 pounds). He was reluctant to release them because the bears had become best friends, and Mike wanted to release them together, but Boo had still not learned to climb a tree. Some research suggests that cubs will often stay together for a few years after leaving their mother.

Mike's methods work well, and to date he has rehabilitated over 50 bear cubs and helped translocate over 80 other bears.

Mike McIntosh owns and operates Bear With Us, a bear sanctuary, using much of his own money to finance the operation.

Harmony, an orphaned bear cub, follows her "mother" Mike McIntosh, as he shows her what is good to eat.

Postscript

I called Mike a year and a half later to get an update. I fully expected that Harmony and Boo would have been released together that fall, but Boo had other ideas. One day when Mike took the cubs for their walk, Boo bolted and was never seen again. Fresh tracks of a small bear appeared the next spring, and Mike wonders if they were Boo's.

He kept Harmony until the following August. She had by then reached the age at which a black bear normally separates from her mother, and she was released north of Algonquin Provincial Park.

35 Vince Shute Wildlife Sanctuary

The sunlight was just filtering down into the meadow when I heard the wolf's distant howl. Not far from where I stood I could see the frosty breath of a large male bear hang in the still air. Another bear glided silently by me, and the wolf howled again.

Mornings like this make up for all the hard work that volunteers at the Vince Shute Wildlife Sanctuary do each day. I had come to this unique place to photograph black bears in their natural habitat and to do a story on the sanctuary. I got much more than I had hoped for during my short stay.

The sanctuary is located about four and one-half hours north of the Twin Cities in Minnesota and an hour south of the Canadian border. I arrived early in August, just in time for the start of the evening's visit. Each night in the summer, the sanctuary opens its gates from 5:00 p.m. to dusk.

Though you won't see bears on the two-mile drive to the parking lot, any disappoint-

The Vince Shute Wildlife Sanctuary is a very special place, supported by donations and manned by volunteers.

This Is A Private, Non-Profit Sanctuary.

We Are Supported By Your Generous Donations

— Thank You —

Below you is a meadow surrounded by forest, and in that meadow are some 50 to 60 black bears. Up in the trees around you, a half dozen cubs wait for their mothers to call them down.

ment quickly changes to excitement, awe, or fear as you make your way down to the green-vested guides who wait for visitors. The instructions are simple: "Stay close together and don't stop to take pictures until we reach the viewing platform." Most visitors strictly obey these instructions, unless they are used to walking past a dozen or so bears, some less than a car length away, each weighing over 250 kilograms (600 pounds).

The short walk takes you to a raised viewing deck that is guarded by a wooden gateway. Once there, you realize why there was no need to stop and take pictures on the way. Below you is a meadow surrounded by forest, and in that meadow are some 50 to 60 black bears. Up in the trees around you, a half dozen cubs wait for their mothers to call them down.

The sanctuary was named after the late Vince Shute (pronounced "shoot-ee"). Back in the early 1940s, Vince came to this land as a logger, and it wasn't long before he had killed his first black bear, attracted by the logging camp's food. He had lost count of the number of bears he killed since then, but reckons the number is in the hundreds. Eventually, he tired of the killing and began to analyze the problem. These weren't bad bears, just hungry bears. To keep them away from camp, he began feeding them in the early 1950s.

At first, the feeding was intermittent, but by the early 1970s he was doing it on a regular basis. Local people started visiting his place to see the bears, and it wasn't long before they were bringing food to feed the bears too. Photographs from those days show a yard littered with old logging machinery, run-down buildings and garbage everywhere. People posed with the bears and even placed their children on the bears' backs—cowboy style—for a picture.

By 1993, Vince's health was failing, and he was concerned about who would keep up the sanctuary and feed "his" bears. There was fear that local "vigilantes" would come in and gun the bears down. There was also real fear in the community that, without Vince to feed them, the bears would start raiding homes and farms.

He had no children to carry on his legacy and there was little interest among the township's residents. It was about then that Bill and Klari Lea entered the picture. Bill is a forester and wildlife photographer from North Carolina. The couple had heard about Vince's bears for several years, but they preferred their bears "wild."

Then they had to deal with managing the two species of large mammals in the area: *Ursus americanus* and *Homo sapiens*.

Visitors are met and instructed on the rules to follow before being escorted to the viewing platform.

They were finally persuaded to visit the sanctuary. There on a four-month leave, it didn't take long for the Leas to see the tremendous potential the site held for educating the public about black bears. The next year, the Lea's agreed to take on the management of the property, legal title was transferred, and The American Bear Association was created. Adopting another common name for the black bear, the American bear, the non-profit organization took over the Vince Shute Wildlife Sanctuary.

Bill and Klari both felt certain changes were required. The garbage-dump feel to the place had to go and twenty thousand tons of garbage were removed, thanks to the help of local volunteers. Then they had to deal with managing the two species of large mammals in the area: *Ursus americanus* and *Homo sapiens*. Bill and Klari didn't want visitors to view the bears as clowns, nor did they want the bears to view the people as food. "I believe these bears are habituated to the site, not to people. You see it in the morning. When a car arrives the bears scatter. It isn't until the evening that they stop paying attention to vehicles," Bill says. It is also a good sign that the bears are very nervous when they encounter anyone outside the main feeding area. Bear management there has developed very well.

"People management" had to be as much a part of the Leas' plan as bear management. They decided to build a viewing stand much like the National Park Service uses in Katmai National Park (Alaska) for the safe viewing of that park's brown bears. While the stand was being built, visitors were asked to keep to a gravel path lined with logs—hardly a barrier capable of preventing crossings by the bears or people.

Many local residents objected to this new confinement. They had fed and wandered among the bears for years, and they resented how outsiders from North Carolina were going to restrict their freedom.

People are now escorted to the viewing stand along a well-defined path. The local residents are slowly accepting the change, and the sanctuary is attracting new visitors to the area who are generally better educated about bears. Most local residents certainly don't mind the new tourism dollars coming into town.

○ Professional photographers are charged a fee for the privilege of working the bears. Restrictions as to where a photographer may shoot help ensure that bears do not encounter people outside the core area.

Local opposition seems to be from two remaining fronts. Hunters object to restrictions designed to minimize bear-human contact. They used to have free range over the land that the sanctuary occupies, and Vince did not object to all-terrain vehicles cutting across his property. This is now actively discouraged. Some hunters also eye the sanctuary's big males as potential trophies. In fact, a year before my visit, a big male, Duffy, was shot only 20 feet from the border. When the Leas and other volunteers ran to see what had happened, the culprits had fled, leaving Duffy's carcass behind.

○ **Hunting Near the Sanctuary**
Bill makes it clear that neither he nor The American

Bear Association is anti-hunting. Some of the volunteers that work there are hunters, others are anti-hunting, but the two sides work together for the bears' benefit. Bill accepts the fact that beyond the sanctuary these bears are hunted, but he thinks that hunting close to the border is unfair. He'd like to see hunters respect the rule of fair chase.

The other group that frets about the bears is the local residents who view bears as a threat to their homes and children. One bear was shot coming through a window after food, though the resident said he hated to shoot one of "Vince's bears." As it turned out, the bear had been fed by another neighbour and was not one of Vince's bears. There are, in fact, several other people that feed bears in the region, but none of these bears are believed to be from the sanctuary.

The year after my visit, Klari proudly reported that all of the large males and adult females had returned to the feeding area for their annual stay. (All the bears are named and their arrivals and departures recorded.) Considering that these bears, especially the big males, are prime targets for hunters, this is quite an achievement. Some of these bears, such as Old Smokey, have been making the trek to the Vince Shute Wildlife Sanctuary for 25 years. Bill doesn't know how far they roam, but one of the Shute bears was trapped and radio-collared recently. "Arrow was caught 100 kilometres (60 miles) from here and he made it back in less than 24 hours. He was obviously traumatized by the experience and came back here where he felt safe." The bear didn't stay long, though. He left after two or three days and has not returned.

Bears begin arriving at the sanctuary in April, but these first arrivals are usually females with cubs-of-the-year. Larger males wait until July, and the numbers peak in early August. At this time there are as many as 80 bears using the feeding area. By late August, the numbers have dwindled, and by October all are gone. Bill has concluded that many of these bears use the sanctuary to bulk up for their winter hibernation. The bears are more aggressive and belligerent towards each other at that time.

Despite the plentiful food available at the sanctuary, the population remains relatively stable at about 80 bears. Sows with cubs make up about one quarter, and the cubs often fail to reappear the next year. Studies have shown that subadult bears are the most vulnerable to predation, accidents, and human-caused deaths (through hunting and car accidents). It is these bears that are most often seen for only a season or two, although some do return year after year. Female bears will sometimes share a portion of their mother's range so these are more likely to reappear than young males. Bill figures the sanctuary is at its "social capacity." By that, he means that the bears have each found a spot in the social structure and that it is very difficult for an outsider to be accepted. New bears do turn up, but few stay long.

Despite the plentiful food available at the sanctuary, the population remains relatively stable at about 80 bears.

○ The most famous of the new bears was an all-white black bear named Halo, but it was removed from the sanctuary due to fear that poachers would want to add a unique trophy to their collection. As a result, the Department of Natural Resources took Halo into "protective custody" before the fall dispersal and then released the bear in a safer region of the state. It is against the law to shoot a white bear in Minnesota unless you are protecting your property.

There are now over 20,000 visitors a year, most of these in the summer. As many as 450 people visit the viewing deck each night.

Bill and Klari take no salary for their time. Like others, they are volunteers. To ensure that the sanctuary does have a full time presence, though, The America Bear Association does have one full-time employee to manage the area. It was looking for an education officer when I was there. The pay is low, and the hours long, but the rewards, if you like bears, are immeasurable.

Volunteers are the backbone of the Vince Shute Wildlife Sanctuary. One man, who came as part of a photo club, now brings one of his sons up with him every weekend in the summer. Other volunteers include a retired teacher and a retired school secretary who Bill somehow convinced to spend the entire summer helping out. There are two sisters who come from New York, a wildlife-photographer, and a professional publicist who was taken with the place when shooting a video at the site.

○ "We need volunteers," Bill told me. "People who can cook, help feed the bears, and guide people in. We can't pay them, and they may have to

look after their own accommodations, but we sure do need them."

University students can apply for an internship that pays 25 dollars a week plus room and board. Along with helping with the chores, they are expected to design a study that will look at some aspect of the area's ecology.

More volunteers are needed from the local community as well. There are now over 20,000 visitors a year, most of these in the summer. As many as 450 people visit the viewing deck each night. There is nowhere else that free-roaming black bears can be viewed in such numbers. Ecotourism could become a growth industry in the region. Bald eagles, white pelicans, and other wildlife are easily spotted in the summer. The sanctuary may turn out to be the crown jewel of this type of tourist destination.

I left the sanctuary deeply touched by both the people and the bears. The Vince Shute Wildlife Sanctuary is a very special place where people and wild animals have learned to co-exist. I hope to return.

36 Whistler's Bears

Arthur Dejong is one of a new breed of what might be called entrepreneur-ecologists. To many the two words represent diametrically opposed positions. Business people concerned with profit margins and the bottom line are not usually at the forefront of the conservation movement. Dejong may well be at the cutting edge of a new way of doing business.

For Whistler's black bears, he has certainly proven his worth.

When I visited with him, Dejong was responsible for practically everything that goes on at

The Whistler complex ranks in the top three ski resorts in the world with over two million visitors per year.

Whistler Blackcomb Ski Resort, located 150 kilometres (90 miles) north of Vancouver, British Columbia. His official title is Whistler Blackcomb Planning and Environmental Resource Manager, which gives him control over both development and the ecology of the slopes.

For most of the year the upper reaches of Whistler Blackcomb are covered with up to three metres (10 feet) of snow. The skiing begins in November and ends in early August with the closing of the Blackcomb glacier site. Most of the area's 200 runs are closed by April or May—just in time for the black bears to come out of hibernation and begin to feed on the greening mountain slopes, particularly the ones used as ski runs.

In the past the bears were often regarded as nuisance animals, and many were destroyed when they visited the town and rummaged through garbage. These killings gave rise to two groups dedicated to improving the town's relationship with the bears—the Jennifer Jones Foundation and the Whistler Black Bear Task Group. Dejong was manager of the ski slopes at the time and was a member of both groups. It didn't hurt that he liked bears and was a confirmed conservationist.

The valley floor, where most of the nine thousand residents live and the two million yearly guests stay, was clearly not a place for bears. That left the mountains, and a large part of their management was left in Dejong's hands. His position had originally been created out of concern for the erosion problem that resulted from the clear cutting for ski slopes. To maintain adequate drainage systems by reducing runoff, the slopes were re-seeded with wild flowers, grasses, and clovers, providing hikers with pleasing views, and not incidentally, providing deer and bears with a source of food that would keep them away from town.

The day Dejong agreed to meet with bear researcher Mike Allen was the turning point in Dejong's vision of the bears' role as an integral part of the Whistler experience. Allen cared deeply for bears and had collected detailed information about those using the resort's slopes, including how many adults and cubs there were and the location of their ranges. Dejong recognized how Allen's work could benefit the bears and the resort, and sought funding to support his research.

Tourists were spotting bears more often as they rode the resort's gondolas to the top of the mountains to enjoy hiking in the alpine meadows. People want to learn more about these animals. Why were they there? Were they dangerous? Allen's research and photographs provided a means of educating the public about black bears and the region's ecology, and a dis-

To address the problem of black bears rummaging through the town's garbage, the Whistler community came up with a successful plan for keeping the bears out of town and on the mountain—with no small thanks to the vision and efforts of Arthur Dejong, Whistler Blackcomb Planning and Environmental Resource Manager.

play was set up in the visitor centre at the top of each mountain.

Although Whistler-Blackcomb is not a park, it is considered important for tourism that it looks like one. Plans now call for the preservation of 55 percent of the slopes as old-growth standing forest, 12 percent glade runs, and 33 percent ski slopes. The more natural the slopes look, especially in the spring to fall season, the better. Wildlife viewing simply enhances the "park-like" experience.

"We believe that we can provide the best mountain experience in the world. Our environmental stewardship and development must reflect this goal," Dejong says. Black bear management and enhancement of their habitat are important parts of the area's seven-point plan. Other goals include increasing waste recycling from the current 35 percent to 50 percent; creating effective green-ups on the slopes; restoring and maintaining water quality; maintaining the balance of forest, glades, and run; and edu-

Thanks to the creative vision of Arthur Dejong, summer visitors to the Whistler Blackcomb Ski Resort often see black bears from the gondola.

Bear viewing has become a successful spring-to-fall tourist draw at Whistler, and Dejong believes that education is an important part of making the experience an enjoyable and safe one.

cating the public. Dejong sees all these goals as attainable while at the same time Whistler offers a quality ski experience in winter and becomes a growing tourist destination in the summer.

He views the resort's relationship with Allen as a symbiotic one. "We need him to monitor the bears and keep us informed. He needs us to support his work." In 2000 their collaboration gave birth to a unique bear-viewing experience. With Allen as the main guide and Dejong filling in from time to time, the resort takes groups of three to four people on 4x4's to view the bears on Blackcomb Mountain. From May to well into July, they achieved a one hundred percent success rate thanks to Allen's knowledge of where the resident nine females tend to feed. Males roam over larger territories, and it is more difficult to predict their locations. For the less adventurous, bears can be spotted from the gondolas.

Toward the end of July, the bears' patterns are less predictable because there is much food available, so the resort switches to offering mountain ecology tours. In late August the bears begin feeding in the huckleberry patches, and the bear tours resume.

Dejong is especially proud of the abundance of huckleberry patches on the mountain, and with good reason—they are there due to his revolutionary approach to designing glades.

When he was a ski patroller several years ago, he was called to rescue a skier from the woods. The more adventurous skiers like to seek out the powder in heavily forested areas. The danger there is very real because skiers must maneuver between trees. On that day, a skier had collided with a tree and died as a result of his injuries.

The memory of this accident prompted Dejong to seek ways to make forest skiing less dangerous. The Ministry of Forestry ultimately agreed to a plan to remove 40 percent of the standing timber to create a narrow glade 50 metres (55 yards) wide. To minimize damage to the environment, the trees were removed either by helicopter or via a cable system. About 20 percent of the cut trees were left in place to promote biodiversity. Like any fallen tree, their rotting hulks provide habitat for a variety of plants, insects, and small mammals.

The results surpassed expectations. Skiers and snowboarders love the newer, safer trails, and new trees and shrubs have regenerated quickly in the now abundant sunlight. The bears now feast on rich huckleberry patches in the glade in late summer. These provide crucial food resources as the bears prepare for hibernation. The cub survival rate is higher here than in the undeveloped mountains, and the number of female bears is expected to increase as female cubs begin to share their mother's home range. Black-tailed deer and their main predator, cougars, have also benefited. As the forest regenerates and saplings grow above snow depth, the existing glade will be closed and a new one created.

Dejong admits that he walks a tightrope balancing development with conservation, but he sees good reason to advocate for both. "If we don't manage our environment and act as good stewards, others will come in and do it for us. This way we control our destiny." He says that the bottom line is still profit. Does the resort benefit? It does—the slopes are enhanced and attract tourists all year round.

And emerging from the tension between developer and conservationist is a better deal for all—more food for the bears, a less hazardous environment for local residents, safer conditions for "extreme" snowboarders and skiers in the winter, more beautiful scenery for tourists in the summer.

Black bear management and enhancement of their habitat are important parts of the area's seven-point plan.

The combination of forest glades and wildflower-covered meadows has proven to be good habitat for the black bears of Whistler.

37 Be Bear Smart

Black bears are a highly adaptive species and continue to flourish in North America. Their search for food brings them close to urban centres, and they are present in or near many major cities, especially on the West Coast. A study in California's San Gabriel Mountains in Los Angeles County reveals that females use their city range in all seasons and are active from dusk to about nine in the morning. Males are more sporadic, leaving the city at times, but when there, will feed mostly in the middle of the night when they are less likely to encounter people.

People can deal with bears in many different ways:

They can seek to eliminate bears by killing them when they turn up in their backyards.

They can ignore bears and allow them to root through their composters and roadside garbage.

They can embrace bears by welcoming them into their neighbourhoods, allowing the bears to den up under their houses and visit their bird feeders.

Or they can do what British Columbia has done—develop reasonable responses to living with bears. Virtually all of B.C. is black bear country, and while it is unlikely that black bears will penetrate to the heart of Vancouver and other major cities, they do frequently show up on the outskirts. The government has taken the lead in implementing a program that encourages communities to become Bear Smart. Whistler is a good example of a town that meets the criteria. Communities are being encouraged to do the following:

1. Prepare a bear hazard assessment of the community and surrounding area.

2. Prepare a bear / human conflict management plan that is designed to address the bear hazards and land-use conflicts identified in the previous step.

3. Revise planning and decision-making documents to be consistent with the bear / human conflict management plan.

4. Implement a continuing education program directed at all sectors of the community.

5. Develop and maintain a bear-proof municipal solid waste management system.

6. Implement Bear Smart bylaws prohibiting the provision of food to bears as a result of intent, neglect, or irresponsible management of attractants, such as garbage.

This program has been so successful that many jurisdictions are creating their own. California's Department of Fish and Game recently began a campaign called Keep Me Wild—Stash Your Food and Trash, aimed at reducing conflict between its burgeoning bear and human populations.

Ontario introduced a program called Bear Wise in 2004. The program came about in response to the growing number of interactions between bears and people, but the real catalyst was the killing of a black bear by an Ontario

Ontario's Bear Wise program has been beneficial to both bears and people.

One part of the solution, rather than killing a bear that is too comfortable in town, is safe removal and relocation.

Provincial Police officer. The young male bear was up a tree in an urban area and was shot—on camera. The footage hit local news broadcasts, and people were horrified. Bear Wise moved forward very quickly and came up with an appropriate response to bears found in urban areas. Only under very specific circumstances (for example, life threatening) can a bear be shot. And the decision would be left to trained "response" personnel, not local police forces.

In 2005 a bear wandered into the city of Markham, in the Greater Toronto Area, and was treed. It was not killed, but tranquilized, captured, and released up north. In 2004 and 2005, black bears have been seen in the suburbs of the Ontario cities of Dundas, Toronto, and Guelph, and even in Buffalo, New York. In fact, just about every city in Canada that lies near bear ranges has had visiting bears, and none have been killed.

In Juneau, Alaska, a similar program focuses on the four E's: Education, Engineering (creating bear-proof containers and fences), Enforcement, and Economy (recognizing the value of bears to tourism and the negative impact of bears on agriculture).

What can you do at your cottage, home, or farm? Follow the steps outlined in this chapter. Identify potential sites where you are likely to have conflict with bears. The way you handle your garbage is the key to getting along with bears. Many areas have moved away from regular curbside waste collection and instead require residents to take garbage to local bear-proof bins that are replaced weekly.

Keep your waste in containers that are bear-proof. Composters are going to attract bears if there is little food in the bush. Should you use one at all? How can you bear-proof it?

Lobby the town to pass and enforce laws against restaurants and food stores having open, accessible garbage containers. Convince the town to require fenced-in garbage dumps and the burning or burying of food that attracts bears.

Most important—educate yourself. The more you understand about bears' behaviour, the easier it is to avoid conflict. By being "bear smart," humans can live together with bears in safety and harmony.

As black bears reclaim their former ranges, we will encounter them more and more. How do we manage this interaction for the benefit of both?

PART IV: Black Bears by Region

Where, exactly, are black bears found in North America, how many are there, and how are they faring? This Part attempts to provide a more detailed view of the state of the black bear in specific areas of North America. The numbers of bears listed in each region are estimates only. Where a range was available, the average number is provided. See Appendices I and II for more detailed data.

38 Eastern Canada

Newfoundland and Labrador: 8,000
Nova Scotia: 8,000
New Brunswick 16,000
Quebec: 60,000

Newfoundland and Labrador, Nova Scotia, New Brunswick, and Quebec

Newfoundland and Labrador

The first documentation of black bears living on the tundra was in Labrador, though there are very few and they have a low reproductive rate, as would be expected from the poor habitat. The fact that they survive there at all illustrates how adaptable the black bear can be.

There are about 6,000 to 10,000 bears living in the province. The island has large herds of moose and caribou, and it was here that one of the first documented studies of black bear predation on ungulate (hoofed mammals) calves took place. The study revealed that the bears are a significant cause of mortality to calves during their first few days of life. Alaska has had similar findings.

Nova Scotia

Nova Scotia reports a population of about 8,000 animals. In the 1970s, the decision to allow bears to be snared and the advent of all-terrain vehicles greatly increased black bear mortality at the hands of humans.

From 1983 to 1987, a little over 90,000 hunters a year obtained deer licences that also allowed them to hunt bears. The average annual kill was about 250 bears. In 1988 separate licences were required, and the number taken dropped to about 60 bears per year, with only about 250 separate bear licences. Before this, between 10 and 20 percent of the estimated population was was killed by hunting. It is now between 2 and 4 percent.

New Brunswick

New Brunswick has one of the largest wilderness areas on the East Coast. It is not surprising that some 16,000 bears roam this province. The number has not varied during the last few years, indicating that the population, despite hunting pressures, is stable. Bears crossing the border into neighbouring Maine have helped bolster that state's bear population. Hunting is allowed, and non-residents are required to hunt with a licenced guide. New Brunswick does have a spring bear hunt.

Quebec

Quebec has approximately 60,000 bears roaming the entire province with the exception of Anticosti Island in the Saint Lawrence River. There have even been sightings in the northern tundra of Ungava Bay, where grizzlies had once lived before the arrival of Europeans.

Bears thrive in the rugged geography of Eastern Canada, which is being opened up by roads leading to mines, electrical generating plants, and logging operations. Farther south, bears can be found literally on the doorsteps of major cities.

In the southern portion of the province, where mixed hardwood forest prevails, there are about 0.5 bears per square kilometre (1.3 per square mile). This figure drops to 0.2 (0.52) in the northern boreal forests, and far less than that on the tundra.

Although it still has a spring hunt, Quebec recently ended its fall black bear hunt in order to increase protection for mothers with cubs. Researchers believe that fall is a more dangerous time for females because in spring, most bears emerge from hibernation in pretty good shape, but in fall, sows either have nursing cubs or are newly pregnant and are far more likely to come to baits because they are hungry. Currently the kill runs to about five percent of the population.

Black bears are common in Gros Morne National Park, Newfoundland.

39 Ontario

Ontario: 100,000

Ontario's black bear population is the second largest in Canada (only British Columbia has more) and the third largest on the continent (Alaska ranks first). There are between 75,000 and 100,000 black bears estimated to be roaming the province's forests.

In recent years black bears in Ontario appear to be slowly expanding their range. Wandering bears, likely young males, have been reported as far south as Toronto. Farther north the bears are re-occupying land previously farmed that is returning to second growth forest.

○ Ontario lays claim to being the original home of one of the most famous bears in the world. Winnie-the-Pooh's creator, A.A. Milne, was inspired by a female black bear cub named Winnipeg. The cub was captured north of Lake Superior in 1914 and donated to the zoo in London, England, where Milne used to take his son, Christopher.

Although technically given the status of a game animal in 1961, the only closed season was during the summer months. This concession was more for the protection of people visiting cottage country—not for the bears. Bears, in the view of the province, were still to be treated as varmints. It wasn't until the 1980s that they were fully elevated to a game species with limited seasons and limited kills. About 1/10th of the province's bears are legally killed each year by between 20,000 and 30,000 licenced hunters.

In Ontario most black bears are hunted over baits. A guide sets out meat, vegetables, or just smelly garbage that attracts bears, who are allowed to feed there for a few days or even weeks. Once the bear has grown accustomed to the spot, a hunter is placed in a stand over the bait and waits until a bear comes in to feed.

○ Algonquin Provincial Park leads all other parks in North America in human fatalities caused by black bears (see Chapter 29 Killer Bears).

Black bear research in the province has been going on since 1961. A study in 1989, conducted in and around the Chapleau Game Reserve, looked at bears of the boreal forest. Its purpose was to determine the differences between hardwood and boreal forest-dwelling bears. It also hoped to determine the number of bears that can be safely removed from a population before the population drops too low to sustain itself. The findings included:

- Female bears living in the hardwood forest reproduce two to three years earlier than do the more northern bears.
- Hardwood bears produce offspring in their sixth year, compared to farther south in the United States where they give birth in their fourth or fifth year.
- Less than five percent of Ontario black

bears are brown or light brown in colour.

- The density of black bears in the study area and in similar areas such as Algonquin Park, where bears are not hunted, was over 60 bears per 100 square kilometres (160 bears per 100 square miles).
- The density of black bears in regions where they are hunted is about 40 bears per 100 square kilometres (100 bears per 100 square miles).

The Ontario studies have helped to confirm the importance of summer and fall feeding to bear survival and reproductive rates. In 1990 when the blueberry crop failed, only 2 of 15 radio-collared females produced cubs. Of 27 cubs sighted that spring, only 13 survived until fall. Evidence pointed to attacks by male bears as the main cause of this loss. It was recommended that female bears should be protected in spring hunts since orphaned cubs have a very low survival rate. Because it is difficult to determine the sex of a bear at a distance, hunters are

Black bears, likely young males, have been seen on the outskirts of Toronto.

urged to wait before shooting to see if a bear is alone—males usually travel this way.

In 1999 the Ontario government passed legislation outlawing the spring bear hunt. Tourism outfitters were caught off-guard by the government's action and lost millions of dollars when booked hunts had to be cancelled. Most of the "lost" hunters were American. The fall hunt remains popular with out-of-province visitors.

Though many people worry about encountering a bear on canoe trips, it is rare to see one. This is the only time the author spotted one while in his canoe, and he was searching for them! The bear's colour provides excellent camouflage in the shadows of the forest.

40 Northern and Western Canada

Manitoba: 27,500
Saskatchewan: 25,000
Alberta: 36,000
Northwest Territories and Nunavut: 5,000

Manitoba, Saskatchewan, Alberta, Northwest Territories, and Nunavut

The three western provinces (not including British Columbia), the Northwest Territories, and Nunavut are treated together because the bear's habitat is very similar.

Manitoba

Manitoba estimates it has between 25,000 and 30,000 black bears living within its borders. Before 1980 the black bear was listed as a predator and could be killed by residents in unlimited numbers. It was then reclassified as a game species and licenced hunting became a significant management tool. Hunters take about 1,200 per year, while trappers remove an additional 400. In order to protect property, another 300 bears are destroyed. Thus, the annual mortality rate is about 2,000 per year. This figure is below the 10 percent figure most jurisdictions feel is the maximum that should be removed. As a result, the bear population in Manitoba is either stable or slowly growing.

Black bears confine their activities to the forested portions of the province. They are rarely found on the Hudson Bay Lowlands. A contributing factor there is likely the presence of large wolves roaming the open boreal forest. These wolves have been seen killing two-year-old polar bear cubs that can be larger than most black bears. There are no black bears living on the prairie.

Saskatchewan

Saskatchewan has between 24,000 and 30,000 black bears, and they are found anywhere in the southern mixed and boreal forests that cover the northern two-thirds of the province. The southern portion of the province is grassland and farms, and has no bears.

○ Of all the provinces, Saskatchewan reported the best bear-viewing opportunities, especially in Prince Albert National Park. Many outfitters will bait bears for hunters and photographers while providing protection as well.

As you move west, either in Canada or the United States, the colour of black bears begins to vary. Studies in Saskatchewan suggest that about one in five black bears are off-coloured bears—brown or cinnamon. Hunting data suggests that 30 percent of the bears here are not black, but it could be that hunters prefer these other colour phases to black ones.

There are no black bears living on the prairie.

Alberta

Alberta had been a leader in black bear management. As early as 1927, bear cubs and females with young were protected, and in 1929 the species was given status as a game animal. This protection was soon repealed, however, when cattle stock losses mounted in the 1930s. It wasn't until 1953 that bear licences were reinstated.

Currently there are some 35,000 to 40,000 bears roaming over 488,000 square kilometres (188,000 square miles) of suitable bear habitat. Their numbers are declining in the mountain parks of Banff and Jasper however. Two reasons have been cited: falling prey to grizzlies and a changing habitat, where the maturing forest no longer suits the bears. Hunters currently take less than 5 percent of the population. The province's goal is to limit hunting losses to no more than 12.5 percent, or roughly 4,500 bears annually.

Northwest Territories and Nunavat

Black bears are common here throughout the boreal forest. They seldom wander onto the tundra, but there have been a few spotted. Black is the most common colour phase. The bears den early here, hibernating by early October. Hunting is allowed, and the limit is one bear, not accompanied by a cub, per year.

○ Because Nunavut's border follows the treeline, it has very few black bears. Nunavut was officially created as a separate territory on April 1, 1999.

Waterton Lakes National Park in Alberta provides excellent bear-viewing opportunities.

41 North America's Northwest

Yukon Territory: 10,000
British Columbia: 140,000
Alaska: 150,000

Yukon Territory, British Columbia, and Alaska

Yukon Territory
There are 10,000 black bears in the Yukon, but this is a paltry number compared to those in Alaska and British Columbia. The Yukon is in the rain shadow of the mountains and gets far less rainfall than the other two. It is colder, has less boreal forest, and more tundra. The black bear population is only slightly larger than that of the grizzly, and both species are managed as game animals and doing well.

British Columbia
Of all the Canadian provinces, British Columbia has the most bears. It is also, geographically, the closest province to the Asian market for illicit bear parts. Bear populations in Asia are being decimated at such a rate that every bear species on the continent is listed as threatened or endangered. Desperate for a new

source, the black marketeers have turned to North America's black bears—many have been poached for their gallbladders. The organs are shipped to China and to North and South Korea for sale for medicinal purposes. The value of some bear parts can be in the thousands of dollars per kilogram (pound).

○ Convention of International Trade in Endangered Species (CITES)
In May 1992, new requirements regarding the transportation of bear parts across international borders were established under the Convention of International Trade in Endangered Species (CITES) mandate. Both Canada and the United States are members of this organization and adhere to its rules. A permit is required in order for a non-resident to transport any part of a bear. These permits are difficult to obtain and the intent is to limit the illegal transportation and sale of bear parts to Asia.

British Columbia has made such poaching illegal and fully supports the CITES ban on transporting bear gallbladders, paws, and genitalia across international borders. Conservation officers strictly enforce anti-poaching laws. It should be noted that virtually every Canadian province between Quebec and B.C. has sustained losses to serve this market.

Still, bears are not threatened in British Columbia. Licenced hunters kill about four percent of the population each year. The bears are found virtually everywhere in the province except on alpine tundra slopes and in major urban communities. Of all areas in North American, only British Columbia can boast having all colour phases. Alaska and B.C. share a part of the blue glacier bear's range, but only British Columbia's northern coastal islands are

British Columbia has published a very complete line of public information brochures on both black and grizzly bears. The Safety Guide to Bears at Your Home notes that every year, 300 to 400 black bears and 10 to 30 grizzlies have to be destroyed because they have become a perceived threat to human life or property. To help prevent these occurrences, several suggestions are made, including:

- Do not feed bears.
- Locate compost heaps, livestock, beehives, and other bear food sources away from thickets and natural pathways used by bears.
- Be watchful of barbecues. The smell from cooking meat attracts bears.
- Keep garbage containers indoors, inside a locked shed, garage, or basement until pick-up day.

The advice should be seriously heeded. There are frequent reports of black bears on the outskirts of Vancouver, British Columbia's largest city. Other pamphlets advise how to control conflict between bears and humans, how to minimize bear problems at industrial camps, and how to maintain personal safety in bear country.

home to the white *kermodei* subspecies. Black bear sightings are quite common, and the province is developing commercial bear-viewing opportunities.

Of all areas in North American, only British Columbia can boast having all colour phases.

Alaska

Alaska leads the continent in bear numbers with about 150,000. They are confined to the forested areas and are seen only rarely north of the Brooks Mountain range. To the south, they are rarely seen on the Seward Peninsula. None are found on the Kodiak archipelago or the large islands of southern Alaska: the main reason—the presence of large numbers of grizzlies.

Sockeye salmon

Along both the British Columbia and Alaskan coasts, black bears and grizzlies can be seen near salmon streams. On such occasions, black bears are usually wary and fish in places where the woods border on a stream. There are reports of large male black bears holding their own against grizzlies, but this would be rare.

Alaska, more than any other state, has promoted bear and wildlife watching. Hunting is allowed and the success rates are high. The black bear population is stable or increasing.

Alaska leads the continent in bear numbers with about 150,000.

This bear, feeding on river grasses, was photographed just outside the town of Whistler, B.C.

The coastlines of British Columbia and Alaska provide excellent opportunities to view black bears in the wild.

42 The Northeast U.S.

Maine: 23,000
Maryland: 300
Massachusetts: 2,000
Vermont: 3,500
Connecticut: less than 45
New Hampshire: 3,000
New Jersey: 700
New York: 5,000
Pennsylvania: 15,000
Rhode Island: less than 10

Maine, Maryland, Massachusetts, Vermont, Connecticut, New Hampshire, New Jersey, New York, Pennsylvania, and Rhode Island

The northeast states include some of the highest human population densities in the country. They boast some very large cities and there is major urban sprawl, yet black bears are thriving in many of these states.

Maine

Maine has the largest number of black bears because it has the largest area of suitable habitat available—over 80 percent of the state—and neighbouring New Brunswick also provides continuous habitat for cross-border "shopping" by the bears.

A large portion of bear country here is second-growth, conifer-deciduous forest, given Maine's history as a logging state. Eastern Maine's spruce-fir forests are particularly well suited because they are interspersed with many blueberry barrens.

Maine put a management plan into place aiming at establishing a viable population of 21,000 to 23,000 bears. Hunting brings in substantial revenue to local and state economies. About 2,000 animals are taken each year by about 10,000 licenced hunters. There has been no negative effect on the population, as it continues to grow. Maine's research program continues, and over 2,000 bears have been radio-collared since research began in 1975. Between 40 and 78 bears are monitored each year and up to 50 winter dens visited.

Maryland

Maryland has about 300 bears, only 1/10th the bear population of Maine, but it too has a management plan in place. Black bears were once common in the state, but by 1850 they had disappeared from all but the western part. No hunting has been permitted there since 1954, and this has allowed the numbers to increase slowly. Some of this increase is also likely a result of successful bear reintroduction programs in Virginia and West Virginia and to Pennsylvania's intensive efforts to expand the bears' range there. Yet, Maryland's black bears are still limited to the western portion of the state.

Increased numbers led to the reclassification of the Maryland black bear from "endangered" to that of a "non-game species of special concern." It has been reclassified again and is now officially a game animal, but no hunting of it is permitted.

○ DNA Study of Fur in Maryland

A recent study in Maryland used DNA samples to estimate the population. Barbwire was run across known bear trails, and when the bears passed under it, fur was collected. Of the 330 samples taken, the researchers were able to identify 92 different bears: 45 males, 42 females, and 5 whose sex could not be determined. The results of this study suggest that Maryland's black bear population is higher than its original estimate.

In 2001 Maryland began a review of its black bear management plan. One of its goals now is to maintain the black bear population at a level based on Cultural Carrying Capacity (CCC). A survey has been undertaken to determine public attitudes toward black bears, which will then influence the optimum target figure. The group's goals included reducing bear-human conflict (between $10,000 and $40,000 per year is paid out to reimburse land owners for bear damage) and ensuring a viable hunting population.

Maryland has the Black Bear Conservation Program, which began in 1986. Supporters of black bears can purchase a "Black Bear Stamp" and the money goes to compensate farmers for bear damage on the property. This is a unique approach to solving one of the most persistent problems of bear management. Beekeepers often bear the brunt of predation by these animals, and programs like this help maintain a balance between the need to both help bears and support agriculture.

Massachusetts

Although once abundant in Massachusetts' forests, the bear was a rare inhabitant by the mid-1950s, and these were probably wanderers from New York and Vermont. Since then the animals have expanded their range, and there is now a breeding population resident in much of the western portion of the state. The season is managed to allow for an annual mortality of 10 to 15 percent. Currently Massachusetts has about 2,000 black bears.

Vermont

Vermont's bears fared a little better in the past, although they too have had their ups and downs. In the 1800s the state's human population grew rapidly, and farming became an important business. Bear numbers declined during this time but they were still common, if not abundant. Since 1900, the trend has been away from farming—over 1.7 million acres of farmland have reverted back to second-growth forests. This has led to an increase in the number of black bears in the state to about 3,500 today. Bears are found statewide with concentrations in the Green Mountains, and are hunted as a managed game animal.

> The black bear's habitat has been affected by the expansion of ski resorts in recent years and an increasing trend for these areas to be used also in the summer.

The black bear's habitat has been affected by the expansion of ski resorts in recent years and an increasing trend for these areas to be used also in the summer. The state, in response, has identified three key habitats in need of protection: hard-mast stands of oak and beech, wetlands, and connecting corridors. A buffer zone of at least 1.6 kilometres (0.5 miles) has been implemented where feasible around these crucial habitats to help bear numbers improve.

Connecticut

Despite the fact that there may be fewer than 45 bears, there is no official designation as threatened or endangered, although no hunting is allowed. Many of the state's bears were likely part of viable populations that wandered in from neighbouring states. These few bears are considered a viable breeding population within the state's borders.

New Hampshire

New Hampshire's black bears have been steadily on the increase since the 1930s. At times, over-hunting caused temporary declines, especially in the mid-1930s and the 1950s, but today an estimated 3,000 black bears are resident and, provided urban encroachment on their range is controlled, they should continue to do well.

New Jersey

New Jersey, one of the smaller states, had only about 50 black bears in 1993. Numbers after that vary. One source estimated 700 for 2003 but the 2005 management plan revised that 2003 estimate to 1,400. This illustrates how difficult it is to get a handle on the actual number of these animals. Black bears inhabit four northwestern counties and appear to be extending their range into at least two others. The management plan laid out recommendations and policies that address several key areas: public education, research, nuisance bear response, and sport hunting. The goal is to maintain a healthy population suitable to the habitat available to them.

Reducing the Number of New Jersey Bear Incidents

In 1999 New Jersey had a record number of black bear incidents reported: 1,607! This was more than double the number reported in 1998 and a very high figure considering the low bear population. The complaints ranged from minor damage to trash containers, to pet and livestock kills. There were 157 reports of property damage, 26 home entries, 21 livestock kills, 13 beehives destroyed, 10 domestic pet rabbits killed, and 7 dog attacks. There were also 30 accidents reported involving bears and motor vehicles. Rising numbers and encroachment by residential development appear to be the major causes of these incidents.

New Jersey's Wildlife Control Unit caught 46 "problem bears," tagged them, and removed them from the area. Before release, the bears received "intensive adverse conditioning" designed to make them think twice before approaching human beings or homes. This behaviour modification program included exposing the bears to the effects of pepper spray, rubber bullets, and pyrotechnics. Repeat offenders were killed. The state also implemented a hunt in 2003 aimed at reducing black bear numbers to about 250 animals in one section of their range. The number of bear incidents that year was 1,308. In 2004 the number of incidents was reduced to 756. Part of that reduction was due to an education program aimed at teaching citizens how to better get along with bears.

New York

New York State has a healthy bear population centered in Adirondack State Park (24,085 square kilometres or 9,300 square miles), which is home to between 4,000 and 5,000 bears. There are also between 500 and 600 bears in the Catskills (3,289 square kilometres or 1,270 square miles) on the southeastern border, and a very small range with 100 to 200 bears in the Allegany Mountains (259 square kilometres or 100 square miles) in the southwest, bordering on Pennsylvania. All three areas represent hilly country where farming was, at best, marginal, and where much of the land has returned to forest. There are between 100 and 300 bears outside these three core areas. There are many bears under the age of one, which indicates a healthy, viable population.

Black bears are hunted in New York State where they have status as a game animal. An average of 689 bears per year have been taken in the decade between 1983 and 1993, mostly in the Adirondacks.

○ In 2002 a five-month-old baby girl was killed in Fallsburg, New York, by a black bear. It was the first time that a black bear had killed a person in the state in living memory. Fallsburg is only 110 kilometres (70 miles) from New York City.

Pennsylvania

Much of the published bear research in the northeast comes from Pennsylvania. Although a heavily industrialized state, there are still regions that provide prime bear habitat. Some of the pioneering research on cub survival and mortality in the den site has been done there.

About 15,000 roam the state (up from 7,500 a decade ago), and it appears that the population is increasing. In at least one area, the bears seem to be coping rather well with urban sprawl. The Pocono Mountain region in northeastern Pennsylvania is well known as a honeymoon retreat, and several large resorts and res-

idential developments have been constructed there since the 1970s, yet the bear population continues to thrive.

The bears are highly valued by local residents and some supplementary feeding also occurs. The state has put in place an extensive live-trapping and removal program to minimize bear-human conflicts. Hunting in the state is a popular sport.

Rachel Carson National Wildlife Refuge, Maine

About 97 percent of black bears in the northeast are in fact black.

Black bears are commonly sited in the Pocono Mountains of Pennsylvania, and some people admit feeding them daily rations of meat.

43 The Southern U.S.

South Carolina: 250
West Virginia: 6,000
Virginia: 3,000
Tennessee: 2,000
Kentucky: 100
North Carolina: 10,000
Georgia: 1,300
Florida: 1,000
Mississippi: 25
Louisiana: 300
Alabama: 50 to 300

South Carolina, West Virginia, Virginia, Tennessee, Kentucky, North Carolina, Georgia, Florida, Mississippi, Louisiana, and Alabama

The bears of the southern United States have not fared well over the past two hundred years. The fact that there are still bears in there at all is a hopeful sign. Some of the South's bear populations are actually doing well, but most are regarded as relic populations, separated from the larger, more viable gene pools to the north. If the bear is to survive there, strong management plans will be required.

South Carolina
A recent study in South Carolina, funded by Clemson University, the U.S. Forest Service, and Duke Power Company, estimates about 200 bears residing in the mountains. These bears roam into North Carolina, Georgia, and Tennessee. There is a one-week hunting season that takes about four or five bears. An unknown number still survive along the coast, with the Myrtle Beach area being one of the most pristine environments and home to a number of black bears. However, these bears are threatened by habitat destruction where homes and industries are being built. The South Carolina Department of Transportation has built six highway underpasses to help reduce fatal bear-car collisions. These man-made corridors (one near Myrtle Beach) have helped reduce bear fatalities and also help other wildlife move freely from one area to another.

West Virginia
West Virginia reports a flourishing black bear population that has been increasing at a rate of about 10 percent per year since 1976. The state holds an annual hunt, which results in a kill of between 400 and 500 bears, although the 1999 number was 696 bears. The population is about 6,000 animals. An ongoing research project in the southern portion of the state continues to monitor the population. As of 2004 almost 400 bears have been handled.

Virginia
Virginia has about half the number of bears as West Virginia. The population appears to be stable or increasing slowly. The state recently completed a relocation project in the southwest counties that took nuisance bears into habitats with low bear numbers. A similar project is proposed for the area south of Piedmont, pending funding. The densest population of bears in

the state can be found in Shenandoah National Park, but it is not easy to spot them.

A study of black bears in the Allegany Mountains of Virginia completed in 2003 concluded that bears there have a higher reproductive rate than the continental average. It also recorded birth dates that were earlier (late December) than those observed in most parts of the range. This was likely due to abundant food and milder/shorter winters. Thanks to both of these factors, black bears are expanding their range there. The state continues to study and monitor the animals, and hunting is allowed.

Tennessee

In 1999 about 2,000 bears lived in the Smoky Mountains of Tennessee, and the numbers are thought to be stable, if not growing. The state is continuing to study the feasibility of maintaining a reintroduced breeding population program in the Big South Fork area on the Kentucky-Tennessee border. In 1996, 14 bears were released into the area. Prior to that only wandering males appeared to be traversing the area—there were few, if any, females spotted.

▼ A Winter Move

Using a release method known as the "winter den technique," females with cubs were removed from their winter dens in the Smoky Mountains and set up in dens in the Big South Fork National Recreation Area. Upon emerging from their new dens, the females and their cubs have a greater tendency to stay in the new area, as opposed to bears released in the summer.

Kentucky

Kentucky has about 100 black bears, but they are mostly wandering two-year-old males and are probably outcasts from established bear populations in neighbouring states. This number is probably low, and no more accurate estimates are available. There had been no documented births in the state for years prior to the implementation of a reintroduction program in Big South Fork National River and Recreation Area in 1996. Twelve radio-collared bears were introduced on an experimental basis to assess the feasibility of a full-scale introduction in the future. The program was deemed a success, and the state continues to assess and monitor its growing black bear population.

North Carolina

North Carolina has a healthy number of black bears—about 10,000, up from 6,200 a decade ago. Currently there are three research projects on black bears being undertaken. Most of the bears are found in the Great Smoky Mountains. Since 1971 black bears have expanded their range from 1 million hectares (2.5 million acres) to over 4 million hectares (10 million acres). Their range now covers coastal plains in the east and mountains in the west. The central portion of the state remains unoccupied. Fueling this expansion was the state's conversion of land from agricultural to urban use. The bears occupied farmland as it returned to bush. Hunting is permitted.

Georgia

The Georgia Department of Natural Resources estimates its bear population at a maximum of 2,000. There are three distinct populations: the Great Smoky Mountains region in the north of the state, a very small area in the centre, and the Okefenokee Swamp in the south along the Florida border. These populations are separated mostly by urban development and highways.

Florida

Historically, an estimated 12,000 black bears once roamed the wilds of Florida. They are now found in 47 of the state's 67 counties, but in virtually all areas they are losing their habitat to Florida's growing human population. Like Georgia, there are several distinct populations, again separated by cities, farms, and highways. Oddly, despite being designated as a threatened subspecies and a recommendation by the Florida Game and Fish Department in 1992 to discontinue hunting, the sport is still allowed in the northern portion of the state.

> Almost 300 bears have been killed on Florida highways—a trend that officials are trying to end by building bear underpasses in areas where accidents commonly occur.

The future does not look bright for Florida's bears. Even today, where the bears are not hunted, mortality is high. On one road alone, State Road 46 near Orlando, 15 of the estimated 1,000 to 1,500 bears in Florida have been killed. Almost 300 bears have been killed on Florida highways—a trend that officials are trying to end by building bear underpasses in areas where accidents commonly occur.

In 1998 the U.S. Fish and Wildlife Agency denied a request to grant Florida black bears the designation of endangered species. The reasons were twofold: there were other, more critically endangered species that should come first, and they estimated the population as higher—between 1,600 and 3,000. Their status review found stable populations in many areas, but Florida argued, unsuccessfully, that the report ignored isolated populations that needed protection.

○ Discrepancies between one agency's population estimate and another's are not unusual. Variations result from different sampling methods, political pressures, and interpretation. All figures should be regarded as rough estimates.

In the swamps of the southeast, black bears cool off in the water, where they will spend the hottest part of the day.

In Great Smoky Mountains National Park a female black bear ambles by a mountain stream looking for insects to eat.

Fortunately, Florida contains the Everglades National Park and several other large state parks and preserves that may help the species survive there. These include Apalachicola National Forest, St. Marks National Wildlife Refuge, Eglin Air Force Base, Ocala National Forest, Osceola National Forest, Pinhook Swamp Wildlife Management Area, and Big Cypress National Preserve.

Mississippi

Mississippi has very few black bears—about 25, plus perhaps 50 that spill over from an isolated Florida population. A few may also wander in from Arkansas. Two hundred years ago Mississippi and Louisiana had an estimated population of over 50,000 black bears between them. The species was listed as endangered in Mississippi in 1984 and a subspecies, the Louisiana black bear, found in the southern half of the state, was listed federally as threatened in 1992. Most of these bears are found along the drainages of major rivers, such as the Mississippi, Pearl, and Pascagoula. Virtually all of Mississippi's bears are believed to be wandering males from other states. There are few, if any females, and there is no indication of any breeding.

Louisiana

In Louisiana's Atchafalya Swamp, the Tensas River Basin, and the Tuncia Hills, the bears hang on, but they are isolated from one another by agricultural lands. There are only between 300 and 350 animals found along the border with Texas. The Black Bear Conservation Committee, a broad-based group of loggers, biologists, landowners, and conservationists, have come up with a plan to return marginal farmland to wooded habitat so that the bears can reunite. Black bears in Louisiana are currently listed as an endangered species.

Alabama

The Alabama Black Bear Alliance was formed in 1999, sponsored mainly by the Alabama Wildlife Federation and The Nature Conservancy. Its mandate is to educate the public about Alabama's black bears and to study bear numbers with the goal of restoring a sustainable population. From research conducted in the Mobile Delta region, it estimates that between 50 and a few hundred black bears live in the state. They exist only in a few isolated swamps and lowlands where the habitat has been heavily logged and is slowly being lost to development. Heavy flooding in the area often destroys dens.

In nearby Arkansas, bear-breeding success is higher, probably due to the presence of large trees that provide denning cavities above the water level. This type of tree is largely missing from the Alabama sites studied.

44 The Central U.S.

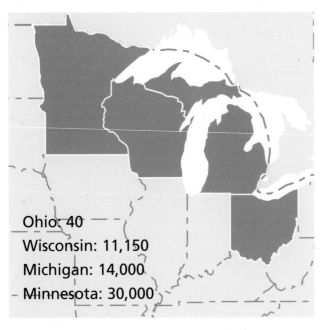

Ohio: 40
Wisconsin: 11,150
Michigan: 14,000
Minnesota: 30,000

Ohio, Wisconsin, Michigan, and Minnesota

The black bears of the central United States have varied success stories. Ohio has barely any, yet those in Michigan, where a management plan is in place, are doing quite well.

Ohio

Ohio's bear population is uncertain. Estimates range from less than 10 to as high as 40. Sightings are on the rise, though, with about 100 reported in recent years. Because most of the sightings are from the eastern part of the state, the bears are probably wandering in from neighbouring Pennsylvania and West Virginia. However, in recent years females with cubs have been spotted, indicating there is now a breeding population in the state. Officially they are classified as a species of "special interest."

This denotes a species that might become threatened or endangered if placed under continued stress. It also marks a species whose status is unknown.

At one time the black bear was common, but, again, farmland and bears do not mix. Bears disappeared completely, and not until the 1970s did they begin to trickle back into their former range. Many of the wandering bears were killed, either by accident or by frightened citizens. Currently, a public awareness campaign is underway and is having a positive effect.

Wisconsin

In Wisconsin the black bear is a familiar resident of the forested region it inhabits. The state has successfully managed the problem of bear-inflicted damage to agricultural interests. Up until 1980, farmers were reimbursed for their losses, but that program was discontinued in favour of a preventative approach that favours other techniques—electric fences, scare devices, repellents, trapping, and translocation. Wisconsin spends about a quarter of a million dollars per year on nuisance-bear programs. On the other hand, bears generate tourism and recreational dollars for the state. The population remains fairly constant at about 11,000 animals. In 2002, 2,400 bears were taken by hunters.

Michigan

Michigan's Upper Peninsula is home to most of the state's 14,000 black bears. Only 1,500 or so are found in the northern portion of the Lower Peninsula. This is largely a reflection of the wilder, less inhabited countryside found farther north. Not surprisingly, there are no black bears in the south where there are large urban and agricultural developments.

Most black bears of the central states are black (*left*), but there are a fair number of other colours represented here as well, such as the one above.

In the late 1980s the state introduced a management program aimed at ensuring the long-term health of the bear population. Bear hunting is limited, and cubs are completely protected. The "harvest" goal is one thousand bears per year. In 1992 and 1993 the kill exceeded that goal by two hundred, but controls are being refined.

Much larger numbers used to roam the state. Records from 1767 show that fur traders shipped 1,142 pelts that year. The continental forces in the American War of Independence wore black bear caps, coats, and robes. It wasn't until 1925 that any hunting regulations were created—anytime of the year was fair game until then.

The continental forces in the American War of Independence wore black bear caps, coats, and robes.

Minnesota

Today, black bears inhabit the northern third of Minnesota. Their range has been greatly reduced since the 1800s by the growth of agriculture and urban sprawl. Until recently they were regarded as a nuisance animal—in 1945 a bounty was placed on them and wasn't removed until 1965. In 1971 the species' economic value was recognized, and it was given status as a game animal. No habitat improvement has been directly undertaken to increase the number of bears, but improvements aimed at increasing Minnesota's deer herd have, no doubt, benefited the bears. Between 14,000 and 17,000 bears were in the state according to a report published in 1998. By 2003 there was an estimated 20,000. The latest figures available (January 2006) show a further increase, bringing the number to 30,000! One reason for this significant increase may be a more tolerant attitude toward the bears (see Chapter 35, Vince Shute Wildlife Sanctuary).

Walk with the Animals

Several studies have been undertaken in Minnesota, the most controversial being the one headed by Dr. Lynn Rogers. He started his work in 1967 in Michigan and later headed a study out of the North Central Forest Experiment Station in Ely, Minnesota, until his retirement a few years ago. Much of what we know about black bears has come from the work done under his supervision. His book, *The Great American Bear*, along with a PBS documentary on his work, created a controversy surrounding the study technique employed. The same technique is used by researchers in Africa, where an animal is followed for 24 hours straight. This works fine on the Serengeti Plains, where the animals can be followed in a vehicle, but in the forests of northern Minnesota, a motorized vehicle was out of the question. Rogers and his students walked with the bears, spending both day and night with them, often within a few metres (yards) or less of mothers with cubs.

The controversy centres around the image that Rogers portrays of bears to the general public. Is this method safe? Would bears normally tolerate such an invasion of their space? The answer is no—not unless you are well trained and very familiar with your subjects. Despite the outcry from concerned naturalist groups, the work continues.

45 The U.S. Prairies

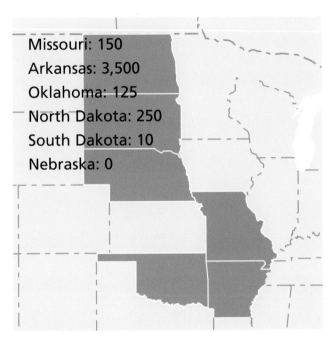

Missouri: 150
Arkansas: 3,500
Oklahoma: 125
North Dakota: 250
South Dakota: 10
Nebraska: 0

Missouri, Arkansas, Oklahoma, North Dakota, South Dakota, and Nebraska

Black bears have never normally been prairie dwellers. The presence of grizzly bears and large buffalo wolves were enough to keep the black bear confined to the woods. When the larger predators were killed off and settlers took their place, the black bear was not considered a welcome neighbour. Although not found on the plains, they did live in isolated islands of mountains: the Ozarks, the Black Hills, and the Ouachita Mountains. Here, with increased elevation, the rainfall was sufficient to support forests that could shelter black bears. For a time the bears flourished here until settlers claimed this land as well.

Missouri
Missouri currently estimates its population at

between 100 and 200 bears. The bears are listed as rare, and a state black bear policy is being developed to better manage these few animals. Although common in the 1800s, they had vanished by the 1930s. This decline resulted from clearing the land for homesteading and logging, especially in the Ozark and Ouachita Mountains that Missouri shares with Arkansas and Oklahoma. By 1894 the black bear was reported extinct. However, a few bears may still have survived.

Some bears have found their way to Missouri from Arkansas, where they had been reintroduced. A 1991 study determined that wandering sub-adult male bears from across the border found and mated with a remnant population of bears that had somehow survived from the turn of the last century.

Arkansas
In the years between 1959 and 1967, the Arkansas Game and Fish Commission successfully re-established black bears in the state. They were able to do so because people were leaving rural areas and the natural habitat had returned to support bears again. The program began with 250 bears back in the 1950s, and there are now 3,500. Over 2,000 are found in the interior highlands, and another 200 are found in the lowlands of eastern Arkansas.

The first group brought in to bolster the existing population came from Minnesota. Forty bears were trapped there and released in the Ozarks. Later, others were brought in, again from Minnesota, and from Manitoba. This re-introduction was so successful that the surplus bears soon began wandering into Missouri and Oklahoma.

Arkansas reports no or few bears in the northern part of the state, while the Ouachita Mountain population is increasing and the Ozark's is stable.

Oklahoma

The population estimate for Oklahoma was between 100 and 150 bears in 1996. A revised estimate placed it at 125 in 2003.

Almost all of Oklahoma's bears reside in the Ouachita Mountains. These bears are the overflow of black bears originally introduced by the Arkansas Game and Fish Commission in the late 1950s and early 1960s. The bears were released into the Ouchia and Ozark Mountains, and as their numbers grew, the bears expanded their range over the border into eastern Oklahoma.

North Dakota

North Dakota has approximately 250 black bears, and these likely emigrated from the forests of neighbouring Manitoba and Minnesota. There is no hunting season for bears here. They are found mostly in the northeast corner of the state in the Turtle Mountains and Pembina River Valley. It is believed that a small breeding population may have been established here. Black bears are completely protected in this state.

South Dakota

Though virtually all prairie, South Dakota does have a small bear population confined to the Black Hills region of the state. There are 10 or so, which may one day form the nucleus of a growing bear population. Two hundred years ago both black and grizzly bears were found here, but both species were extirpated by the early 1900s.

Nebraska

Nebraska reports only the occasional sighting of black bears, and these are believed to be wandering males from South Dakota's Black Hills. The species was considered extinct in the state with the last official sighting occurring in 1907. In 1984 a black bear was seen in the western portion of the state. Another sighting was reported in 2000 and one more in 2002. Anyone seeing a bear is encouraged to report it to the Nebraska Game and Parks Commission.

Black bear numbers are increasing in the plains states as wildlife agencies employ new techniques to help out these animals.

46 The Northwest U.S.

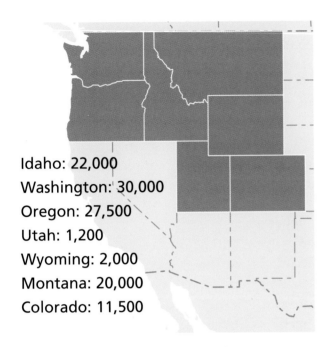

Idaho: 22,000

Washington: 30,000

Oregon: 27,500

Utah: 1,200

Wyoming: 2,000

Montana: 20,000

Colorado: 11,500

Idaho, Washington, Oregon, Utah, Wyoming, Montana, and Colorado

All of the northwestern states have healthy black bear populations. A few even have remnant populations of grizzly bears in the more remote and protected areas. These six states account for over 100,000 of the continental United State's black bear numbers.

In all of these states, the black bear is a prized game animal, often hunted on the same licence as elk, moose, mountain sheep, and goat. There are a number of national and state parks, wildlife refuges, and game reserves that protect the black bear and its habitat.

Not surprisingly, there is much hostility directed toward bears here—this is cattle country, or at least much of it is, and black bears do kill domestic animals. Loggers, too, have little use for them—they kill trees by stripping off the bark. They also raid beehives as well as agricultural crops. Overall, they are viewed as pests.

On the other hand, tourism is big business here, and bears are a popular draw. Montana and Wyoming are both on the "Trail of the Great Bear," a tour initiative that includes parts of the Canadian west as well. State legislatures, caught between these competing interests, have developed programs that try to address the concerns of both groups.

Idaho
Idaho has a variety of black bear habitats spread over nearly 85,000 square kilometres (33,000 square miles). The estimated population is over 22,000 and appears to be increasing. Hunting seasons in the state are controlled. Nuisance animals that cause damage to the state's agricultural interests are usually removed, either through trapping or hunting.

The state's management goals include maintaining and improving black bear populations and distribution, offering a variety of hunting and recreational opportunities, collecting better data on the economic and social values of black bears, and reducing conflicts between competing bear user groups.

Washington
Washington leads the continental United States in black bear numbers. An estimated 30,000 roam the state. Though it is home to a few grizzlies, state game officials estimate there are seven hundred black bears for every one grizzly. That's a real sleuth of bears. Until the 1970s black bears were killed in large numbers to control damage done to young Douglas fir trees on which the bears fed. Since ending this control measure and instituting regulated

hunting seasons, black bear numbers have rebounded. In 1996 public concerns over bear hunting led to the elimination of hunting with hounds and by means of baiting. Bear numbers increased and management plans are in place to limit people-bear confrontations.

Oregon

Oregon ranks next after Washington in terms of highest numbers of black bears with 27,500. Though most of these bears are black coloured, about 20 percent represent other colour phases comprising various shades of brown. Officially there are no grizzlies in the state, although rumors persist that some wandering grizzly bears may be there. Like all states with large numbers of black bears, Oregon has developed a bear management plan to ensure the safety of both humans and bears.

Utah

Utah's 1,200 bears seem like a small population by comparison. Still, that number is double the estimate in the mid-1970s, so it is clear the population is healthy and occupying the limited habitat suitable for it. The species has been protected here since 1967 when a group of sportsmen petitioned the Utah state legislature to protect both the cougar and the bear. This led

to both species gaining game animal status and a management plan was put into place. Prior to this, bears and cougars were classed as vermin and could be hunted any time. The spring bear hunt was eliminated in 1993.

In one Utah study of black bear scats, it was found that less than three percent of the scats contained animal matter. Mule deer remains (faun teeth were present) were the most common mammal represented (in 9 of 859 scats analyzed). Other mammal remains included black bear, cattle, domestic sheep, rock squirrel, cottontail rabbits, and three other species of small rodents. It is likely that the cattle fed upon had died of other causes than direct predation.

Wyoming and Montana

Both of these states are unique in the U.S. in that they have viable and increasing populations of grizzly bears. Because the grizzly is a "species of concern," it is heavily managed and information is quite accessible. Statistics for Wyoming's black bears are harder to find, but a published report in a national hunting magazine suggests there are 2,000. They are confined to the forested areas found in the Rocky and Bighorn Mountains. Yellowstone National Park is a prime spot for black bear viewing.

Black bears in both these states are managed as a game species. In 2004 about 294 black bears were taken by hunters in Wyoming. Both Wyoming and Montana have spring bear hunts and monitor the number of female bears killed. If the number exceeds the quota established by wildlife managers (too many females to maintain a sustainable population), fall numbers are adjusted to compensate for the loss. About 1,000 bears are killed each year in Montana. On average, a third of these are female.

Black bears in the west come in the greatest variety of colours thanks, in no small part, to the wide variety of habitats available to them.

Montana has more black bears than Wyoming with the population estimated to lie between 17,000 and 20,000. This is due to more abundant forest cover. A recent incident where a grizzly bear was "mistaken for a black bear" and shot has led to a Be Bear Aware program to help hunters correctly identify the species (grizzlies are protected). The program, begun in 2005, has "Stormin Norman"—General H. Norman Schwarzkopf—as its spokesperson. Both states offer online bear quizzes on their websites.

Colorado

Colorado has been studying its black bears since 1979. Like the other states, it has been attempting to balance the landowners' concern with destruction of property, the hunters' desire for a game animal, and the public's positive attitude toward bears in general. The first group tends to take the position that no bears are too many; the next has the attitude that bears are a natural resource to be hunted; the third wants all bears preserved.

It was clear that no one solution would satisfy everyone. Colorado responded, like many other states, by developing a compromise that would ensure a stable and perhaps growing black bear population. Hunting regulations were put in place with specific target groups of bears, usually males, and seasons were limited. Increased anti-poaching enforcement units were set up, and the sale of any part of the bear is prohibited. Critical bear habitat is protected, landowners' losses are reimbursed, and offending animals are removed.

Public education is also high on the state's lists of goals. The state encourages the development of opportunities for bear viewing, while publications keep interested individuals abreast of the latest sites.

Current estimates put the bear population at about 11,500, which are found in areas with suitable habitats in the western two-thirds of the state. The highest population densities occur in the montane shrublands from Walsenburg and Trinidad west to the San Luis Valley, in the San Juan Mountains, and in the canyon country of west-central Colorado.

Some of the longest and earliest studies of black bears were conducted in the American west. The animals are valued here as both a game species and a tourist attraction.

47 The Southwest U.S.

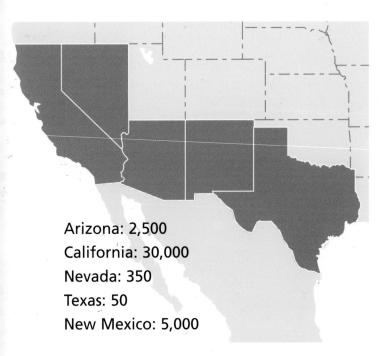

Arizona: 2,500
California: 30,000
Nevada: 350
Texas: 50
New Mexico: 5,000

Arizona, California, Nevada, Texas, and New Mexico

Arizona

Arizona's black bear population appears to be stable at about 2,500 to 3,000 animals. Most are confined to the forested peaks of high mountains. Droughts sometimes force them to leave these areas to seek out food around cities and towns. Bears that reach the Phoenix area likely use wildlife corridors along the Verde and Salt Rivers. Sightings are rare, as black bears here, like everywhere else, are excellent at avoiding people.

Although much of southern Arizona appears to be desert and therefore unsuitable for black bear habitat, pockets of mountains trap moisture and support lush meadows and pine forests. Ski resorts are a good place to look for black bears during the spring green-up when the bears feed on the slopes.

California

California's bear population has increased since 1985, when strict laws governing the hunting of bears and the use of hounds were introduced. The species is considered common throughout the forested portion of the state. In the northwest, densities of 0.75 bears per square kilometre (2 per square mile) have been reported. The current estimate is about 30,000.

> Yosemite was well known in the 1970s and 1980s for its "mugging" bears—they would confront hikers on a trail, who would drop their backpacks, leaving the bears with food.

Black bears are often spotted in Redwood, Sequoia, and Yosemite National Parks.

Yosemite was well known in the 1970s and 1980s for its "mugging" bears—they would confront hikers on a trail, who would then drop their backpacks, leaving the bears with food. The park went to considerable lengths to revert the bears back to more normal behaviour. It implemented its Human-Bear Management Plan in 1975 to educate people about bears, clean up potential areas of conflict (garbage

The return of the black bear to portions of its former range, particularly in Texas, is hailed as a great achievement in conservation.

containers, food storage sites), and enforce regulations against feeding of all wildlife. It seems to have worked.

Nevada

Nevada only has about 350 black bears, mostly in the mountains of the western portion of the state. The population was thought to have decreased by the early 1990s, with poor winter snow cover and a growing human population cited as the causes. The most recent estimates suggest that the numbers have more than doubled in the decade between 1990 and 2000, but accurate figures are difficult to obtain in Nevada's rugged terrain. There is no hunting season.

Texas

There are even fewer bears in Texas—only about 50—which survive in Guadalupe Mountains National Park and Big Bend National Park. Big Bend has had more sightings—the estimated population is still only 20—and plans are underway to ensure their survival.

Black bears roamed widely throughout the state until the early part of the last century, but by the 1950s they were all but gone. In 1973 the hunting season for bears was closed, and in 1987 the bear was given official status as a state endangered species.

It appears that black bears are entering the

eastern part of the state from Louisiana, and Mexican bears are moving north into the area around Big Bend. In 1987 the Mexican government banned black bear hunting. This was followed by several good breeding seasons in which food was plentiful, and the bears expanded their range across the Rio Grande.

Despite the low numbers, campers in Big Bend National Park, as well as sheep and goat ranchers nearby, have reported problems. Since 95 percent of land in Texas is privately owned, the public's tolerance is essential if the black bear is to survive as a resident of the Lone Star State.

In 2005 the Texas Parks and Wildlife Department began the process of developing the East Texas Black Bear Conservation and Management Plan. It will be implemented over the next 10 years. Its intent is to manage and restore suitable black bear habitat for the purpose of re-establishing the bear as a viable part of the native wildlife community of east Texas.

> Since 95 percent of land in Texas is privately owned, the public's tolerance is essential if the black bear is to survive as a resident of the Lone Star State.

In the 1970s and 1980s, Yosemite's bears were too people-smart. They would intimidate hikers and break into cars for food.

New Mexico

New Mexico gave its black bears game status in 1927, but its bear population is declining. A research study completed in 2001 determined that there were more bears than previously estimated, between 5,000 and 6,000. They are found, for the most part, at higher altitudes. Such areas also include prime recreational land, and bear-human encounters do occur. Droughts also bring bears into residential areas—and conflict with people. Like most jurisdictions, New Mexico continues to develop programs and plans to better manage bear-human conflict.

○ The most famous black bear in the U.S., Smokey the Bear, was a New Mexican black bear cub found suffering burns from a forest fire. The ensuing publicity led the U.S. Forest Service to adopt the bear as a symbol in 1950.

Yosemite National Park

Appendix I

United States Black Bear Numbers by State

State	1966	1977	1993	2000	2003
Alabama	0	50	150	150	150
Alaska	20,000	45,000	150,000	150,000	150,000
Arizona	0	700	1500	2750	2500
Arkansas	200	900	2330	3000	3500
California	22,000	13,000	20,000	20,000	31,000
Colorado	8200	5,000	10,000	10,000	11,500
Connecticut	0	0	30	30	45
Delaware	0	0	0	0	0
Florida	450	450	1000	1500	1000
Georgia	500	500	1000	2000	1,300
Idaho	8000	17000	22,500	22,500	22,500
Illinois	0	0	0	0	0
Indiana	0	0	0	0	0
Iowa	0	0	0	0	0
Kansas	0	0	0	0	0
Kentucky	20	12	100	100	100
Lousiana	200	400	300	300	300
Maine	7,000	8,500	20,000	23,000	23,000
Maryland	0	0	200	200	300
Massachusetts	8	85	700	1,800	2,000
Michigan	5,500	6,500	8,000	12,000	14,000
Minnesota	10,000	10,000	10,000	20,000	20,000
Missouri	12	70	75	100	150
Mississippi	20	20	25	50	50

State	1966	1977	1993	2000	2003
Montana	6,500	8,500	17,500	17,500	20,000
Nebraska	0	0	0	0	0
Nevada	0	24	300	300	350
New Hampshire	800	800	800	3000	3,000
New Jersey	12	12	40	550	700
New Mexico	1,500	3,000	4,000	5,500	5,000
New York	1,250	4,000	4,500	5,000	5,500
North Carolina	1,000	1,000	6,200	9,500	10,000
North Dakota	0	0	250	250	250
Ohio	21	10	10	40	40
Oklahoma	25	50	200	125	125
Oregon	10,000	15,000	25,000	27,500	27,500
Pennsylvania	1,000	2,300	7,500	10,000	15,000
Rhode Island	0	0	4	4	4
South Carolina	250	150	200	300	250
South Dakota	0	0	10	10	10
Tennessee	250	400	1,250	2,000	1,250
Texas	50	50	50	50	50
Utah	500	500	900	1,000	1,200
Vermont	2,000	1,500	2,200	2,750	3,500
Virginia	2,000	1,500	3,000	3,500	3,500
Washington	35,000	27,000	27,000	30,000	30,000
West Virginia	800	600	3,500	6,000	6,000
Wisconsin	2,750	7,000	6,000	13,750	11,150
Wyoming	2,000	2,000	2,000	2,000	2,000
Totals	**151,784**	**185,560**	**362,317**	**412,109**	**434,077**

Note: Where a range was available, the average is provided. In all cases these are estimates only. The only population estimate provided for Oklahoma for 1966 was zero but this was likely an error, so an estimate of 25 has been substituted.

Appendix II

Canadian Black Bear Numbers by Province and Territory

Province	1966	1977	1993	2000	2003
Alberta	na	100,000	40,000	37,000	36,000
British Columbia	na	100,000	120,000	140,000	140,000
Manitoba	na	na	28,000	27,500	27,500
New Brunswick	na	na	15,000	13,500	16,000
Newfoundland	na	3,000	7,500	8,000	8,000
Northwest Territories/Nunavut	na	na	6,000	5,000	5,000
Nova Scotia	na	na	2,500	8,000	8,000
Ontario	na	90,000	70,000	87,500	100,000
Quebec	na	na	60,000	60,000	60,000
Saskatchewan	na	35,000	30,000	25,000	25,000
Yukon	na	4,000	10,000	10,000	10,000
Totals	**na**	**333,977**	**390,993**	**423,500**	**437,503**

Note: Where a range was available, the average is provided. In all cases, these are estimates only. No data exists for Canadian black bear numbers for 1966, but the population was likely at least equal to and possibly twice that of the United States. Thus, the Canadian figure would be roughly 200,000 for that year.

Appendix III

Parks, Preserves, and Sanctuaries

The following areas all offer a chance to view black bears. If the area is a park or wildlife reserve, letters should be addressed to the superintendent. In many cases the address is a company name that offers tours.

***** guarantees success
**** virtually guarantees success
*** excellent chances of success
** may see a bear
* bears are present but success not assured

Most ratings are based on the author's experience. Some ratings are based on information supplied by government agencies or tour companies. No rating means the author did not visit the location and insufficient information was available. Rates for tours vary from under one hundred dollars to well over one thousand.

Canada

Algonquin Provincial Park** Superintendent, P.O. Box 219, Whitney, Ontario, R0J 2M0, (705) 633-5572, e-mail: info@algonquinpark.on.ca

Banff National Park** c/o Superintendent, P.O. Box 900, Banff, Alberta, T0L 0C0, (403) 762-3324

Bruce Peninsula National Park ** P.O. Box 189, Tobermory, Ontario, N0H 2R0, (519) 596-2233, e-mail: bruce-fathomfive@pc.gc.ca

Duck Mountain Provincial Park* Manitoba

Glacier National Park P.O. Box 350, Revelstoke, B.C., V0E 2S0, (250) 837-7500

Grass River Provincial Park* Manitoba

Gwaii Haanas National Park, Reserve and Haida Heritage Site*** P.O. Box 37, Queen Charlotte, B.C., V0T 1S0, (250) 559-8818

Jasper National Park Box 10, Jasper, Alberta, T0E 1E0, (780) 852-6176, e-mail: JPN_info@pc.gc.ca

Kejimkujik National Park and National Historic Site Box 236, Maitland Bridge, Annapolis County, Nova Scotia, B0T 1B0, (902) 682-2772

Kootenay National Park P.O. Box 220, Radium Hot Springs, B.C., V0A 1M0, (250) 347-9615, e-mail: kootenay.reception@pc.gc.ca

La Mauricie National Park** 702 5th Street, P.O. Box 160, STM Bureau-chef Shawinigan, Quebec, G9N 6T9, (819) 538-3232, e-mail: parcscanada-que @pc.gc.ca

Mount Revelstoke National Park** P.O. Box 350, Revelstoke, B.C., V0E 2S0, (250) 837-7500, e-mail: revglacier. reception@pc.gc.ca

Pacific Rim National Park and Reserve** 2185 Ocean Terrace Rd., P.O. Box 280, Ucluelet, B.C., V0R 3A0, (250) 726-7721 e-mail: pacrim.info@pc.gc.ca

Prince Albert National Park (Western Arctic Field Unit)*** P.O. Box 100, Waskesiu, Saskatchewan, S0J 2Y0, (306) 663-4522 or toll free 1-877-255-7267, e-mail: PANP-INFO@pc.gc.ca

Princess Royal Island** B.C. c/o Adventure Canada, Suite 105, 227 Sterling Road, Toronto, Ontario, M6R 2B2, (416) 533-0767 or Suite 100, 1159 West Broadway Ave., Vancouver, B.C., V6H 1G1M, (604) 736-7447

Riding Mountain National Park Wasagaming*** Manitoba, R0J 2H0, (204) 848-7272 or toll free 1-800-707-8480k e-mail: rmnp.info@pc.gc.ca

Tofino **** Vancouver Island, B.C.

Waterton Lakes National Park*** Superintendent, Alberta, T0K 2M0, (403) 859-2224

Whistler/Blackcomb Resort, B.C. ****

Whiteshell Provincial Park, Manitoba,

Yoho National Park P.O. Box 99, Field, B.C., V0A 1G0, (250)343-6783, e-mail: yoho.info@pc.gc.ca

United States

Adirondack State Park and Preserve** New York

Anan Creek**** Jo Van Os Photo Safaris, Box 655, Vashon Island, WA 98070, (206) 463-5383

Big Bend National Park* P.O. Box 129, TX 79834, (432) 477-2251

Big South Fork* 4564 Leatherwood Road, Oneida, TN 37841, (423) 286-7275

Black Canyon of the Gunnison National Monument* Park Headquarters, 102 Elk Creek, Gunnison, CO 81230, (970) 641-2337

Blue Ridge Parkway** 199 Hemphill Knob Road, Asheville, NC 28803-8686, (828) 271 4779

Delaware Water Gap National Recreation Area** HQ River Road off Rt 209 Bushkill, PA 18324, (570) 588-2452

Everglades National Park* 40001 State Road 9336, Homestead, FL 33034-6733, (305) 242-7700

Glacier National Park** Park Headquarters, PO Box 128, West Glacier, MT 59936, (406) 888-7800

Grand Canyon National Park* P.O. Box 129, Grand Canyon, AZ 86023, (928) 638-7888

Grand Teton National Park P.O. Drawer 170, Moose, WY 83012-0170, (307) 739-3300

Great Dismal Swamp National Wildlife Refuge* Virginia

Great Smoky Mountains National Park** c/o Superintendent, Gatlinburg, TN 37738, (615) 436-5615

Isle Royale National Park* 800 East Lakeshore Drive, Houghton, MI 49931-1895, (906) 482-0984

Kings Canyon National Park* 47050 Generals Highway, Three Rivers, CA 93271-9700, (559) 565-3341

Lake Clark National Park and Preserve** c/o Superintendent, 701 C Street, P.O. Box 61, Anchorage, AK, (907) 271-3751

Mount Rainier National Park** Tahoma Woods, Star Route, Ashford, WA 98304-9751, (360) 569-2211

North Cascades National Park** 810 State Route 20, Sedro-Woolley, WA 98284-1239, (360) 856-5700

Olympic National Park** 600 East Park Avenue, Port Angeles, WA 98362-6798, (360) 565-3130

Ozark National Scenic Riverways, 404 Watercress Drive, PO Box 490, Van Buren, MO 63965, (573) 323-4236

Redwood National Park*** c/o Superintendent, 1111 Second Street, Cresent City, CA 93257, (707) 464-6101

Rocky Mountain National Park* 1000 Highway 36, Estes Park, CO 80517-8397, (970) 586-1206

Sequoia National Park*** 47050 Generals Highway, Three Rivers, CA 93271-9700, (559) 565-3341

Shennadoah National Park** 3655 U.S. Highway 211, East Luray, VA 22835-9036, (540) 999-3500

Superior National, Forest** c/o Superintendent, P.O. Box 338, Duluth, MN 55801, (218) 727-6692

The Poconos** Pennsylvannia

Vince Shute Wildlife Sanctuary***** The American

Bear Association, P.O. Box 77, Orr, MN 55771

Yellowstone National Park** P.O. Box 168, WY 82190-0168, (307) 344-7381

Yosemite National Park*** c/o Superintendent, P.O. Box 577, CA 95839, (209) 372-4461

Viewing Lodges and Tours

Riding Mountain Guest Ranch
Box 11, Lake Audy, MB, R0J 0Z0
(204) 848-2265
wildlifeadventures@escape.ca
www.countryvacations.mb.ca/ridingmountain
www.wildlifeadventures.mb.ca
Season: Summer through mid-September

Knight Inlet Lodge
c/o Knight Inlet Lodge, 8841 Driftwood Road, Black Creek, BC, V9J 1A8
(250) 337-1953
http://www.grizzlytours.com/index.html
grizzly@island.net
Season: Spring through fall. Contact them directly for best viewing times for bears.
Comments: Black bears are often viewed right from the lodge.

Discover Charters and Lodges
PO Box 48, Quathiaski Cove, BC, V0P 1N0
(near Tofino on Vancouver Island)
1-800-668-8054,
http://www.discoverychartersandlodge.com
info@discoverychartersandlodge.com

Silver Salmon Creek Lodge
c/o David and Lee Coray, Box 3234, Soldotna, AK, 99669 (Lake Clark National Park)
(907) 262-4839
Season: Summer
Comments: Black and grizzly bears

Granite Park Chalet
Belton Chalets, Inc, Box 188, West Glacier, MT, 59936 (Glacier National Park)
(406) 888-5511
Season: Summer through fall
Comments: Good chance of bears but they may be in distance. You must hike in.

Many Glacier
Glacier Park Inc., Box 146, East Glacier, MT, 59434
(406) 226-5551
Season: Summer through fall
Comments: Black and grizzly bears. Bears might be seen from road or along trails.

Glossary of Terms

abiotic: non-living things in an environment (examples include fire, water, longitude, latitude, the amount of sunlight, starlight, moonlight, soil, rock, location, and climate)

adapt: change to meet the conditions of the surrounding environment

adaptation: specific ways in which an organism (living thing) has changed to become suited to its environment

alpine: occurring at high altitude, between the tree line and the permanent snow line

ambush: a method of hunting that involves hiding and waiting for prey to come to the hunter

amphibian: an animal that has skin, a backbone, and is cold-blooded. (Most amphibians lay eggs and go through a larval stage such as the tadpoles of a frog.)

antler: a bony structure found on the head of deer

arboreal: living in or mainly in trees

archosaurs: a major group of reptiles that includes dinosaurs, pterosaurs, crocodiles, and birds

artiodactyl: any hoofed animal

atmosphere: the envelope of gases that surrounds Earth (consists of the following gases: 78% nitrogen, 21% oxygen, less than 1% argon, 0.03% carbon dioxide, and small quantities of other gases)

avoidance: behavior that allows an animal to escape danger or conflict

bacteria: a diverse group of single-celled organisms

bark: the protective layer of trees and bushes

behavior: what living things do

biologist: a scientist who studies biology

biology: the study of living things

biomass: the weight (mass) of living things in an area

biotic: living things in the environment including animals, plants, fungi and single-celled organisms

blastocyst: a fertilized egg that is not attached to the uterine wall

blood: the fluid in which nutrients, oxygen, and waste products are dissolved and carried around the body

bruin: informal term for a bear

calorie: a measure of the energy available in food. (Calorie with a capital C stands for 1,000 calories and is the measure used in this book. One Calorie = 4.182 Kilojoules. A calorie is also a measure of the amount of heat required to raise the temperature of water one degree Celsius.)

camouflage: coloration or patterns that allow animals to hide in their environment

Canadian Shield: an area of granite rock that encircles all but the northern portion of Hudson Bay. (It consists of some of the oldest rock in the world.)

canine teeth: the sharp, pointed teeth of mammals. Humans, monkeys, apes, and carnivores all have canine teeth.

carbon: a non-metallic element that is the basis for all life

carbon dioxide: a colourless, odourless gas that is a waste product of respiration and is used in photosynthesis

carbohydrates: food formed during photosynthesis containing the elements of carbon, hydrogen, and oxygen

carcass: the remains of a dead animal

carnassial teeth: specially adapted teeth found in mammalian carnivores. They consist of the last upper pre-molar (P4) and the first lower molar (M1).

Carnivora: scientific term used to describe the order carnivore. These are placental mammals possessing carnassial teeth.

carnivore: commonly used to describe any meat-eater, it also refers to a specific group of related mammals (bears, raccoons, hyena, cats, dogs, weasels, and mongooses)

carnivorous: an animal that eats mainly meat

carrion: the remains of a dead animal

cellulose: the framework of cell walls in a plant

climate: the average weather conditions of a region

cold-blooded: animals that do not control their body temperature but that rely on the temperature of their surroundings

common: the species is not threatened or of concern

competition: a type of behaviour that goes on between two or more living things that require the same resource (food, water, mate, space)

conservation: protecting our natural resources, including animals, from being destroyed

consumer: an organism that must eat or consume another organism for its food or energy

copulation: mating

courser: an animal that runs down its prey

courtship: behaviour that takes place prior to mating

creodont: an extinct order of mammal having shared a common ancestor to the carnivores

Cretaceous Period: the third period of dinosaur rule from 135 to 65 million years ago

cud: the thicker material that floats to the top of the rumen; the material a ruminant re-chews

deciduous: referring to a family of trees that have broad leaves which are lost every autumn (for example, maple or beech)

decomposers: organisms that break down the remains of living things into their basic elements

defecate: passing solid waste (for example, droppings, scat, or stools)

detritus: the partially decomposed remains of living things

digest: to go through the process of digestion

digestion: the process by which complex molecules in food are broken down and absorbed into the body and used as energy sources

dinosaur: a special type of land reptile with an erect gait; a member of the archosaur group that lived between 224 million and 65 million years ago

dominance: to be higher ranked (as in the bull is dominant over the cow) or to be more common (as in grasses are the dominant species)

drought: a long period without any rainfall

ecologist: a scientist who studies the ecology of an ecosystem

ecology: the study of living things and their relationship to each other and their environment

ecosystem: a complex system of living (biotic) and non-living (abiotic) things in a specific area (for example, the boreal forest of North America)

endangered: likely to become extinct

endangered species: living things that may become extinct in the near future unless given immediate help and protection

endothermic: warm-blooded; being able to produce body heat and maintain a constant temperature

equator: an imaginary line running east and west around the centre of Earth that divides Earth into two equal halves or hemispheres. The equator is 0 degrees latitude

estrus cycle (also oestrous cycle): the hormonally controlled reproductive cycle in many female mammals

evaporate: to convert to vapour (gas)

evolution: change over time

evolve: to change to become better suited to the changing environment

excretion: a waste product; the result of metabolism that includes urine, feces, and gases

external parasite: flies, insects and other "bugs" which live on the blood of an animal or which lay their eggs on its hide or in its nose

extirpated: extinct in a specific location, but not extinct as a species

extinction: a species no longer capable of reproducing; a species that no longer exists

fast: to go without eating for an extended period

fawn: a baby deer

feces: solid waste (droppings, stool, or scat)

fertile: capable of producing offspring

food chain: consists of three levels; plant, plant eater, and meat eater (there may be more than one level of meat eater)

forage: food eaten by grazing animals (for example, grass); searching for food

genus: a taxonomic classification of animals, plants, and all living things having common characteristics and containing several species

geography: the study of Earth's surface and its related physical, biological, and cultural features

geology: the study of Earth's rocks, minerals, and physical formations

germinate: to grow from a seed

granite: a hard, coarse-grained igneous rock

grass: any of 9,000 species in the monocotyledonous family *Poacea*. These plants have leaf sheaths split lengthwise on the opposite side of the blade. The stem is cylindrical and hollow between the nodes.

grassland: an area, usually extensive, dominated by grasses

grazer: a large animal that eats primarily grass

habitat: the surroundings in which an organism lives

habitat loss: the prime cause of species disappearing on Earth

habituated: refers to animals used to human contact

hemisphere: the world is divided into halves (north of the equator is the northern hemisphere; south of the equator is the southern hemisphere)

herbivore: a plant eater

hibernation: the winter sleep of animals

hierarchy: the social order of animals

hormone: a group of chemicals released by the body which control growth and sexual maturity

hyperphagia: the feeding binge of bears prior to hibernation

igneous rock: rock formed under great heat and pressure below the surface of Earth

ingestion: the process the eating or consuming of food

internal parasite: an organism that lives inside another organism

introduced: a species that has been returned to an area where it was extirpated or into an area where it was never found

kilocalories: the standard (U.S.) unit by which scientists measure energy. (A calorie is equal to 4.2 kilojoules.)

kilojoules: the metric unit in which scientists measure energy

larva: the immature wingless form of many insects

marsupial: a primitive mammal that gives premature birth to its young and then nurses it in a pouch (for example, kangaroos and opossums)

mast: a crop of nuts or berries born seasonally, usually by trees

mating: the breeding of a male and female pair of one species

Mesozoic period: "Middle Life"; it lasted from 225 to 64 million years ago

midden: food storage area of a squirrel or mouse; also a term applied to a regular area of dunging by some species marking territories; also a storage area of the pack rat

migrate: to move from one place to another, usually for food or to mate

minerals: chemicals found in the ground that are necessary for healthy bodies

niche: the role an organism fills in an ecosystem

nocturnal: active at night

nutrients: chemicals found in food which are necessary for a healthy body

oestrous cycle: (also estrus cycle) the hormonally controlled reproductive cycle in many female mammals

omnivore (omnivorous): an animal that eats both plant and animal matter

order: a taxonomic ranking between the rankings of class and family. All organisms within an order will share similar characteristics.

ovulate (ovulation): the biological function of releasing an unfertilized egg as part of the reproductive cycle

oxygen: a gas vital to most life forms on Earth; a waste product of photosynthesis

parasite: a plant or animal that lives off another living thing and does it harm (for example, fungi)

parasitic: the act of harmfully living off of another organism without benefiting it in any way

peccary: a distant relative of the wild pig

photoperiodism: the timing of biological events related to the amount of sunlight and the angle of that light

photosynthesis: the process by which plants convert the sun's energy into plant matter

placenta: a flattened, circular organ that provides nourishment through the umbilical cord to unborn young

plantigrade: a way of walking in which the whole sole or palm of the limb is touching the ground. Bears and humans are plantigrade species.

poaching: the illegal killing or taking of an animal for food or profit

population: the number of one species living in a given area

precipitation: rain or other forms of moisture falling from the sky

predation: behavior that involves one species killing and eating another

predator: an animal that hunts and kills other animals for food

prey: an animal that is hunted by a predator

protein: the building blocks of life; any of a class of highly complex nitrogenous (nitrogen-based) organic compounds originally synthesized by plants, and after hydrolysis by enzymes, turned into amino acids, forming an essential part of the processes of animal metabolism

Quaternary period: second period of the Cenozoic era that lasted from 2 million years ago to the present

rain shadow: the area of land where air masses descend after dropping rain and snow as they climb over mountains; the air warms and picks up moisture, dropping very little

rain forest: a forest where precipitation is very high

range: the area in which a species can be found

receptive: a female that is willing to accept a mate

reproductive rate: the rate at which a species reproduces

respiration: the process in plants and animals whereby oxygen is taken from the air and / or water and carbon dioxide is released as a waste by-product

rodents: a family of mammals which have large front teeth used for gnawing

rumen: the first stomach of a ruminant

ruminant: a mammal that chews a cud, such as cattle, deer, sheep, goats, and antelope

saggital crest: raised part of the skull that anchors muscles

scatologist: a scientist who studies animal scats (droppings)

scatology: the study of animal scats (droppings)

scavenger: an animal that lives off the dead remains of plants and animals

seed shadow: the area over which a bear (or other seed eater) deposits its seed-bearing scats

sleuth: a "herd" or group of bears

species: organisms that can reproduce their own kind; a distinct animal or plant group that shares similar characteristics and can produce offspring within its group

species of concern: a species that scientists feel might be threatened or that could become threatened, but for which there is little data or research available

suckle: the act of nursing from a mother's teats

symbiosis: (symbiotic) a close association between two species that benefits both

temperate: a climate that is moderate throughout the year; located between the Arctic Circle (66°33′N) and the Tropic of Cancer (23.5° N), and the Tropic of Capricorn (23.5° S) and the Antarctic Circle (66°33′S)

territorial: a behavior related to acquiring a territory

territory: an area that an animal claims and defends as its own, usually contain the food, water, and shelter the animal needs. In the case of a female, it must also provide for her offspring.

threatened: a species that may become endangered if immediate action is not taken to save it

ungulate: a mammal that has hooves

urinate: passing urine

urine: a liquid waste product of the body; a fluid excreted by the kidneys

uterine wall: the wall of the uterus where the fertilized egg is attached during development

vole: a small rodent resembling a mouse, with a shorter, hairy tail and smaller eyes and ears

vulva: female sex organ

vulnerable: a species that may become threatened if action is not taken to help it

Alaska. *Alaska's Wildlife: Guide to Wildlife Watching in Alaska.* Department of Fish and Game, 1991.

Alaska Department of Fish and Game website: http://www.adfg.state.ak.us

Bauer, Erwin A. *Bear In Their World.* New York: Outdoor Life Books, 1985.

Bear Trust Website: http://www.beartrust.org

Bear Wise Website: http://bears.mnr.gov.on.ca/

Beecham, John J. "Population Characteristics of Black Bears in Central Idaho." *J. Wildlife Management* 47.2 (1983).

Beecham, John J., D.G. Reynolds, and M.G. Hornocker. *Black Bear Denning Activities and Den Characteristics in West Central Idaho.* Int. Conf. Bear Research & Management. 5:79 86, 1986.

Behler, Deborah. "Black Bear Trade Curb." *Wildlife Conservation* Ju/Aug 1992. New York: Zoological Society, 1992.

Bittner, Steven L., *Estimating Maryland's Black Bear Population.* Maryland DNR Wildlife & Heritage Service, 2002.

Britton, Barbara, and Jonquil Graves. *Black Bears and Grizzlies of the Northwest Territories.* NWT Dept. of Renewable Resources, 1985.

Bromley, Marianne. *Safety in Grizzly and Black Bear Country.* NWT Dept. of Renewable Resources, 1986.

Brown, Tom. *Tom Brown's Field Guide to Nature Observation and Tracking.* New York: Berkley Books, 1983.

Bibliography

Cardoza, James E. *The History and Status of the Black Bear in Massachusetts*. Massachusetts Division of Fish & Wildlife, 1976.

Cardoza, James E., M. Sayre, and K. Elowe. "Black Bears in Massachusetts." *Massachusetts Wildlife* XL4, fall 1990.

Clark, Joseph D. "Ecology of Two Black Bear Populations in Arkansas". Diss. U of Arkansas, 1991.

Clark, Joseph D., Djuro Huber, and Christoper Serveen. *Bear Reintroductions: Lessons and Challenges.* (Invited Paper)

Clarke, Stephen H. *The Black Bear in New York State*. New York State Dept. of Environmental Conservation Educational Leaflet, 1977.

Cooke, Steve. "Hunting." *Ontario Out of Doors Magazine* April 1993.

Cox, Daniel J. *Black Bear*. San Francisco: Chronicle Books, 1990.

Centre for Wildife Information: Be Bear Aware website: http://www.centerforwildlife information.org/BeBearAware/ bebearaware.html

Craighead, Frank. *Track of the Grizzly*. San Diego: Sierra Club, 1979.

Crawford, John S. *Wolves, Bears and Bighorns*. Anchorage: Alaska Publications, 1980.

Cronan, John M., and Albert Brooks. *The Mammals of Rhode Island*. Rhode Island Dept. of Natural Resources, 1968.

Dawson, Blair. "Science Scan." *Ontario Out of Doors Magazine* June 1992.

Domico, Terry and Mark Newman. *Bears of the World*. New York: Facts On File, 1988.

Dood, Arnold R., et al. Final Programmatic Environmental Impact Statement: The Grizzly Bear in Northwestern Montana. Montana Dept. of Fish and Wildlife, 1986.

East, Ben. *Bears*. New York: Crown Publishers, 1977.

Elbrocht, Mark. *Mammal Tracks and Signs: A Guide to North American Species*. Mechanicsburg, Penn.: Stackpole Books, 2003

Eliot, John L. "Tunnels: Low Road to Safety for Florida Black Bears." *National Geographic* 183.5 May 1993.

Ennis, Connor. "Bear Kills 5-Month-Old Girl in N.Y." The Associated Press 8/20/02.

Fair, Jeff and Lynn Rogers. *The Great American Black Bear*. Minocqua, Wisconsin: Northword Press, 1990.

Fischer, Carol and Hank. *Montana Wildlife Viewing*. Billings, Montana: Falcon Press, 1990.

Garner, Nathan P. and Thomas Mathews. *Black Bear Management Plan (1992–2001)*. Maryland Dept. of Natural Resources, 1992.

Geist, Valerius. "Pronghorns, Fires and Fossils." University of Alberta, 1.1, 1988.

Gill, R. Bruce. *Black Bear Management Plan 1990–1995*. Colorado Div. of Wildlife Report 15, 1990.

Graham, Patrick J. *Management of Black Bears in Montana*. Montana Dept. of Fish and Wildlife, 1994.

Gunther, Kerry A. *Yellowstone National Park Bear-Related Injuries/Fatalities*. Information Paper No. BMO 1, Yellowstone N.P., Wyoming, 1993.

Heacox, Kim. "Alaska's Yellowstone." *Wildlife Conservation* 97.2 (1994).

Henckel, Mark. *The Great Bear*. Billings Gazette, Montana.

Herrero, Stephen. *Bear Attacks: Their Causes and Avoidance*. Toronto: McCelland and Stewart, 2003, 1985.

Idaho. *Grizzly Bear Recovery in the Bitterroots*. Dept. of Fish and Game, 1993.

Jolicoeur, Helene. *Black Bear Hunting and Trapping in Quebec*. Ministere du Loisir, de la Chasse et de la Peche, Quebec, 1992.

Kerr, John. "Bear Kills Timmins Man." *Ontario Out of Doors Magazine* Aug. 1992.

King, Judith E. *Seals of the World*. New York: Comstock Publishing, 1983.

Knight Richard R. and L.L. Eberhardt. "Population Dynamics of Yellowstone Grizzly Bears." *Ecology* 66.2 (1985): 323–334.

Krammer, Kari. " Make Way for Black Bears." *Country World*: East Texas ed., Feb. 24, 2005.

Kynaston, Suzanne and Paul Ward. *Bears of the World*, London, England: Cassel Plc, 1999.

LeBlanc, P.J., M.E. Obbard, B.J. Battersby, A.K. Felskie, L. Brown, P.A. Wright, and J.S. Ballantyne. "Correlations of plasma lipid metabolites with hibernation and lactation in wild black bears Ursus americanus." *Journal of Comparative Physiology* B171 (2001): 327–334.

Lynch, Wayne. *Bears: Monarchs of the Northern Wilderness.* Vancouver: Douglas & McIntyre, 1993.

MacDonald, David. *Carnivores: All The World's Animals.* New York: Torstar, 1984.

Maine Department of Inland Fisheries and Wildlife. *Bear Facts.* http://mainegovimages.informe. org/ifw/old_but_keep/bear_refer endum/bearfacts.pdf

Marion, Catherine and Remy. *On the Trail of Bears.* Hauppage, NY: Barrons Nature Travel Guides, 1998.

Marty, Sid. "Ghosts of the Rain Forest." *Canadian Geographic* Feb. 1993.

Maryland Department of Natural Resources website: http://www.dnr.state.md.us/

MassWildlife website: http://www.mass.gov.

Mattson, David J. *Human Impacts on Bear Habitat Use.* Int. Conf. Bear Research and Management 8:33–56, 1997.

McLaughlin, Craig R., et al. *Maine Status Report-Eleventh Eastern Black Bear Workshop.* Maine Dept. of Natural Resources, 1992.

McLaughlin, Craig R. and Kenneth D. Elowe. *Beechnuts & Bruins.* Maine Fish and Wildlife, 34.3 (1992).

Michigan. *Black Bear Management Planning for the Year.* (draft) Dept. of Natural Resources, 2000.

Michigan. *The Bear Facts: Michigan's Black Bear.* Dept. of Natural Resources, Wildlife Division, 1990.

Mills, Enos A. *The Grizzly.* New York: Ballantine Books, 1919.

Mills, Judy. "The Sum of Their Parts." *Pacific Discovery* 47.1 (1994).

Minnesota Department of Natural Resouces website: http://www.dnr.state.mn.us

Mississippi Department of Wildlife, Fisheries and Parks website: http://www.mdwfp.com/wildlifeissues/default.asp

Montana Fish, Wildlife and Parks website: http://fwp.mt.gov/wildthings

Montana. *Grizzly Bear Recovery Plan.* Fish and Wildlife Service, 1993.

Murie, Olaus. *A Field Guide to Animal Tracks.* Boston: Houghton Mifflin, 1954.

National Park Service website: http://www.nps.gov

National Wildlfie Federation website: http://www.nwf.org

Nebraska Game and Parks Commission website: http://www.ngpc.state.ne.us/wildlife

Neilsen, Barbara. "Swamp Bear." *Wildlife Conservation* July/Aug. New York: Zoological Society, 1992.

New Jersey state website: http://www.state.nj.us

New Jersey. *Upland Wildlife and Furbearer Research, IX—Black Bear Research.* Dept. of Environmental Protection, Division of Fish and Game, 1992.

New Mexico State University website: http://spectre.nmsu.edu

New York State. *Hunting the Black Bear in the Adirondacks.* Dept. of Environmental Conservation.

Nobbe, George. "Bear Bones Wildlife." *Wildlife Conservation* July/Aug. New York: Zoological Society, 1992.

North Carolina Wildlife Resources Commission website: http://www.ncwildlife.org/

Northern Prairie Wildlife Research Center website: http://www.npwrc.usgs.gov/index.htm

Novak, Milan et al., ed. *Wild Furbearer Management and Conservation in North America,* Ontario Ministry of Natural Resources, 1987.

Obbard, Martyn E. *Black Bear Ecology.* Ontario Ministry of Natural Resources, 2001.

Obbard, Martyn E. and George B. Kolenosky. *Seasonal movements of female black bears in the boreal forest of Ontario in relation to timber harvesting.* Int. Conf. Bear Research and Management, 9:363, 1994.

Obbard, M.E., G.D. Campbell, and A. Schenk. "Evidence for fatal injury inflicted on a female black bear by a moose." *Northeast Wildlife* 55 (2000): 57–62.

Olsen, Jack. *Night of the Grizzlies.* New York: Signet, 1969.

Oregon Department of Fish and Wildlife website: http://www.dfw.state.or.us

Outdoor Alabama website: http://www.outdooralabama.com

Peacock, Doug. "Walking Point in White Bear Country." *Pacific Discovery,* 47.1 (1994).

Pederson, Jordan C. *Utah Black Bear Harvest 1992.* Utah Dept. of Natural Resources Publication # 93–1, 1993.

Poulin, Rovay (chair), Martin Obbard, et al., *Nuisance Bear Review Committee, Report and Recommendations,* Ontario Ministry of Natural Resources, 2003.

Powell, Daniel. "Research Update Year 3." *Alabama Wildlife Magazine* winter 2000.

Rearden Jim. *Alaska Mammals.* Anchorage: Alaska Geographic, 1981.

Rennicke, Jeff. *The Smoky Mountains Black Bear: Spirit of the Hills.* Gatlinburg, Tennessee: Great Smoky Mountains Natural History Ass., 1991.

Rezendes, Paul. *Tracking and the Art of Seeing.* New York: HarperPerennial, 1999.

Richard, B. *Performance Report: Job No. 68: Black Bear Status.* Texas Fisheries and Wildlife Division, 1991.

Riley, Laura and William. *Guide to the National Wildlife Refuges.* New York: Collier Books, 1992.

Russell Andy. *Grizzly Country.* New York: Alfred A. Knopf, 1967.

Schullery, Paul. *The Bears of Yellowstone.* New York: Roberts Rinehart, 1986.

Scott, Keith. *Hiking in Bear Country.* Halifax: Nimbus Publishing, 1995.

Stafford, Robert W. Personal correspondence. California Dept. of Fish and Game, 1993.

Stephenson, Marylee. *Canada's National Parks: A Visitor's Guide.* Toronto: Prentice Hall, 1983.

Stirling, Ian. *Bears: Majestic Creatures of the Wild.* Emmaus, Pennsylvania: Rodale Press, 1993. Stirling, Ian. *Polar Bears.* Toronto: Fitzhenry & Whiteside, 1989.

Stone, Karen D., and Joseph Cook. "Phylogeography of black bears (Ursus americanus) of the Pacific Northwest." *Canadian Journal of Zoology* 78(2000): 1–6.

Stowell, Laine R. and Robert C. Willging. *Bear Damage to Agriculture in Wisconsin.* Proc. East. Wildl. Damage Control Conf. 5.96–104, 1992.

Strickland, Dan. *Raven (Algonquin Park Newletter),* Ontario Ministry of Natural Resources, April 23, 1992.

Taylor, Dave. *Algonquin Park: Excursions with a Photographer.* Toronto: Natural Heritage Press, 1994.

Taylor, Dave. *Endangered Mountain Animals.* Mississauga, Ontario: Crabtree Press, 1992. Taylor, Dave. *Ontario's Wildlife.* Erin, Ontario: Boston Mills Press, 1988.

Taylor, J. David. *Game Animals of North America.* Toronto: Discovery Books, 1987.

Taylor, J. David. "Ontario's Killers In Black." *Ontario Out of Doors* March 1981.

Taylor, J. David. "Ontario's Polar Bears." *Ontario Out of Doors* March 1984.

Tedford, Richard H. "Key to the Carnivores." *Natural History Magazine,* 103.4, New York: American Museum of Natural History, 1993.

Texas Parks and Wildlife. *East Texas Black Bear Conservation And Management Plan 2005–2015,* website: http://www.tpwd.state.tx.us

Titus, Russ (chair). *An Interim Management Plan for Black Bears in Missouri (Draft IV).* Missouri Department of Conservation, 1993.

Trauba, David. "Black Bear Population Dynamics, Home Range, and Habitat Use on an Island in Lake Superior." diss. U of Wisconsin, 1996.

Trout, John, Jr. "To Fear or Not to Fear." *Bowhunter Magazine,* Apr-May 1994.

United States Department of Transportation (South Carolina Department of Transportation) website: http://www.fhwa.dot.gov/environment/ecosystems/sc05.htm

United States Geographical Survey website: http://pubs.usgs.gov

United States. *IGBC Briefing Paper on Grizzly Bears.* Interagency Grizzly Bear Committee, 1993.

Utah. *Utah Black Bear Management Plan.* Division of Wildlife Resources 00.23, 2000.

Van Wormer, Joe. *World of the Black Bear.* New York: J.B. Lippincott, 1966.

Virginia Department of Game and Inland Fisheries website: http://www.dgif.state.va.us/.

Visser, Larry G. and Carl L. Bennett, Jr. *Tetracyline: A New Approach for Marking Bears.* Michigan Dept. of Natural Resources, 1990.

Visser, Larry G. and Tim F. Reir. *Michigan Status Report.* Michigan Dept. of Natural Resources, 1990

Wallace, Tom. "Bowhunter Bear Forecast 1994." *Bowhunter Magazine,* Apr-May, 1994

Washington. *1991 Status Report Endangered & Threatened Wildlife.* Dept. of Wildlife, 1991.

Washington Department of Fish and Wildlife website: http://wdfw.wa.gov

West Virginia Dept. of Natural Resources website: http://www.wvdnr.gov/.

Wilkinson, Todd. *Yellowstone Wildlife: A Watcher's Guide.* Minocqua, Wisconsin: Northword Press, 1992.

Willey, Charles H. *The Vermont Black Bear.* Vermont Fish & Game Dept.

Williams, Martin. "Beside the Panda." *Pacific Discovery* 47.1 (1994).

Wilson, Don and Sue Ruff. *The Smithsonian Book of North American Mammals*. Washington and London: Smithsonian Institution Press, 1999.

Wilson, Mary. "Bear Gardens." *Pacific Discovery* 47.1 (1994).

Wolgast, Leonard J. et al. *Comprehensive Black Bear Management Policy*. New Jersey Fish and Game Council, 2005.

Wyoming Game and Fish website: http://gf.state.wy.us

Index